CONTENTS

Out of the Fog . . .

SOMETHING FOR NOTHING

ARBITRAGE AND ETHICS ON WALL STREET

MAUREEN O'HARA

W. W. Norton & Company
Independent Publishers Since 1923
NEW YORK | LONDON

Printed in the United States of America
First Edition

For information about special discounts for bulk purchases, please contact W. W. Norton Special Sales at specialsales@wwnorton.com or 800-233-4830

Manufacturing by Berryville Graphics
Book design by Brooke Koven
Production manager: Anna Oler

ISBN 978-0-393-28551-2

W. W. Norton & Company, Inc.
500 Fifth Avenue, New York, N.Y. 10110
www.wwnorton.com

W. W. Norton & Company Ltd.
15 Carlisle Street, London W1D 3BS

1 2 3 4 5 6 7 8 9 0

PREFACE

THE IMPETUS FOR this book came at a breakfast meeting I had with an acquaintance a little over three years ago. My breakfast companion was a very accomplished practitioner who had been asked to teach a short college course on finance. He wanted advice on teaching materials that incorporated ethics in teaching basic financial concepts. My response was that finance wasn't taught that way—that net present value, option pricing, arbitrage, and the like are tools and that we teach students how to use them analytically. He wondered whether if we taught that way students ever learn (or even ask) about when it was appropriate to use these tools. I had no particularly good answer.

Since then I have incorporated more focus on ethical issues in finance in my own classes. Of course, events in the financial crisis and its aftermath also made the need to do so more pressing. These classroom discussions highlighted for me both the complexity of these ethical issues and the importance of trying to focus not only on how to do things but also on when to do them. Perhaps more important, I realized we needed to spend even more time on the why we do them—and on why finance can be used to make markets and society better-off. I also think we need to have these discussions more broadly, not just in academic settings but in the public forum as well.

I decided to write this book because I think those issues are both interesting and important. Modern finance is complicated, and even understanding how some of the more complex contracts work can be baffling to practitioners, let alone to students, regulators, journalists, and the public. Sorting out the ethical dimensions can be more challenging still, in part because not everyone shares the same ethical perspective. But even when there is general agreement on that front, those finance-related ethical issues often arise in the context of firms and markets, where the ethical dimensions become ever more opaque. I found that even among my more finance-literate friends there was often strong disagreement about what does and does not "cross the line." For those less well versed in finance, the answers were actually more uniform—whatever the financiers were doing was wrong!

I hope this latter view is not correct, and in this book I have tried to take the reader on a journey toward sorting this out. Certainly, I have enjoyed trying to put ethics and finance together, and puzzling through the various case studies made me appreciate just how challenging all this can be. Perhaps some readers will share my views on where the lines are drawn, but I suspect there may be others who completely disagree. What I hope is apparent to all is that ethics and finance cannot live in separate spheres—and that debate on these issues can only be to the good.

I do know the importance of getting this right. Unfortunately, I now have firsthand knowledge of what can happen when even one individual opts to cross the line and the repercussions it can have on a firm. I currently serve on several corporate boards, and at the time of writing this manuscript was the chairman of the board of a global broker-dealer firm. We found ourselves dealing with a Securities and Exchange Commission (SEC) investigation. The particular issue, which led to a settlement with the SEC, involved what the board of directors believed was a limited pilot project that would be completely regulatory compliant and meet all required disclosures. In fact, an outside review by an independent law firm concluded that, unbeknownst to the board of directors, clearly articulated company policies were violated. That the violation happened five years ago and was shut down, that some in the firm did the right thing in catching and stopping the behavior, cannot undo the disappointment felt by the eleven hundred employees at the firm who always strived to put clients first. We worked to rectify the situation, but it would have been far better if the behavior that caused this had never happened in the first place.

Many of the themes I develop here can be found in other work, and I freely admit to being influenced by a wide range of authors. Some, such as Robert Shiller in his thoughtful book *Finance and the Good Society*, make the case for why finance can be a source for good. Others, such as Raghuram Rajan and Luigi Zingales in their book *Saving Capitalism from the Capitalists: Unleashing the Power of Financial Markets to Create Wealth and Spread Opportunity* or Jonathan Macey in his book *The Death of Corporate Reputation: How Integrity Has Been Destroyed on Wall Street*, raise prescient warnings about emerging problems in capitalist systems. Still others, such as the *Economist* magazine article "Greed—and Fear," make the case for why finance has failed and why arbitrage played a role in that failure. As will be apparent in the discussions throughout this book, a wonderful resource on ethical frameworks is the "Justice" course offered on edX by Michael Sandel (and his many related books and articles on the subject). John Bogle's superb book *Enough: True Measures of Money, Business, and Life* should be required reading for all—particularly those who fear that greed is the only motivator on Wall Street.

I also greatly benefited from extensive discussions with a wide range of people. I am very grateful to Jim Detert for his guidance on behavioral ethics, Michael Brennan and Joe Kaboski for their broad knowledge of ethics and philosophy, Brandon Becker and Jonathan Macey for insights on the many legal dimensions, David Easley for thoughtful discussions on economics, and Chidozie Ugwumba for valuable research assistance. I also thank participants at the Lumen Christi conferences at the University of Chicago for spurring my interest in these general issues, and the many people who offered assistance or read earlier chapters, including Robert Battalio, William Christie, Abby Joseph Cohen, John Frishkopf, Robert Jarrow, Marcos Lopez de Prado, Hamid Mehran, Thomas Noone, Dana Radcliffe, Rafe Sagalyn, Jamie Selway, and Steve Strogatz.

Finally, I am particularly grateful to my two editors at Norton. I consider myself very fortunate to have had the honor of working with Jack Repcheck, whose encouragement and excellent suggestions really made this project work. His untimely death was a loss to so many, including this author. I am obliged to Brendan Curry for stepping in to help with the final manuscript, and especially for his many thoughtful suggestions. Both Brendan and I hope Jack would have been proud of this book.

SOMETHING FOR NOTHING

CHAPTER 1

FINANCE, ARBITRAGE, AND ETHICS

In 2001, Goldman Sachs structured a complex financial contract so that its client, the government of Greece, would appear to have far less debt than it actually did. This allowed Greece to satisfy the Maastricht guidelines on deficits and so meet the requirements for inclusion in the eurozone. When news of this transaction came out in 2010 after the onset of the European sovereign debt crisis, uproar ensued. Angela Merkel declared, "It is a scandal if it turns out that the same banks that brought us to the brink of the abyss helped to fake the statistics." *Business Week* referred to Greece and Goldman as "two sinners."[1] Other observers pondered whether Greece (and Goldman) had used the tools of modern finance to deceive the market.[2] Was this behavior ethical?

The furor surrounding this case reflects a growing concern that modern finance is not good for society. The view that sophisticated financial instruments enhance the overall performance of the economy has been replaced by the suspicion that finance diverts resources that would be better used elsewhere. Joined to this are misgivings that finance has only served to enrich the few at the expense of the many. The seemingly endless number of scandals at financial firms, combined with the perception that financial alchemy simply allows the already rich to steal from the unknowing, has solidified wariness into mistrust. From Occupy Wall Street to the *Economist* magazine, the question raised is whether the golden age of finance has turned into the failure of finance.

There is a lot that is disquieting. But I think the current blanket denunciations of finance miss the point. The tools of finance are not the problem. What is a problem is that some finance practitioners have lost sight of when it is appropriate to use those tools.[3] Modern finance often involves arbitrage, or the use of financial tools to remove price differences for identical things trading in different markets. At a simple level, arbitrage entails "buying low and selling high," thereby forcing prices back into equilibrium. At a more complex level, arbitrage uses financial tools to remove inefficiencies more generally, for example, by creating a less expensive way to borrow money than is possible with existing contracts. The recent development of securitized solar energy bonds providing cheaper financing for renewable energy projects illustrates this broader application.[4]

When arbitrage is done right, it can lead to tremendous benefits to the economy, allowing resources to go to their best uses at essentially little or no cost (in effect, getting "something for nothing"). But these same financial tools can be used to exploit others, to take advantage of the complexity in modern markets to behave unethically. When that happens, practitioners have missed the simple notion that "just because you can does not mean you should." In short, the problem lies in the intersection of arbitrage and ethics.

That ethics plays a role in arbitrage activities may seem obvious to some people and incomprehensible to others. Searching for a price discrepancy in a market, and then buying low and selling high is simply a strategy—it is not a moral judgment. But, increasingly, it seems that practitioners may not even consider that some uses of arbitrage-based strategies are inappropriate, that there are limits on what is acceptable in markets and society short of what is simply illegal. Being able to profit from arbitraging inefficiency is not ethical if it takes unfair advantage of others—as happened, for example, when JPMorgan Chase's traders profited by taking advantage of the opacity and complexity of the California electricity market auction system to essentially get paid for not producing electricity! (We discuss the specifics of what they did in chapter 7.) But what exactly is "unfair"? We would all probably agree that exploiting the financially naïve (the proverbial widows and orphans) is not acceptable, but discerning this unfairness more generally in modern capital markets is far more complicated. Decrying a lack of ethical culture misses the larger problem that exactly what is unethical is not readily apparent to a surprising number of people on Wall Street and on Main Street.

I believe we need to think more carefully about these issues—to recognize both that there are lines and where these lines might exist. In this book, I make the case for why some arbitrage-based activities cross those lines. By making it clearer how modern finance works, I hope to reduce the confusion surrounding financial activities, making it easier to appreciate both why modern finance can be used to make society better-off and why, if misused, it can have the opposite effect. By suggesting some general ethical frameworks (as well as some behavioral pitfalls), I hope to provide a basis for recognizing ethical boundaries. And, by examining a variety of recent financial scandals, I hope to illustrate when these lines were crossed. I fully expect some (maybe all) readers will disagree with where I draw these lines, but thinking through this disagreement is exactly the introspection I hope to foster. As Scott Adams so artfully described, we are venturing into the "weasel zone: the giant gray area between good moral behavior and outright criminality."[5]

Before we can draw the lines between weasels and felons, between what is clever and what is simply exploitative, we must first understand how modern finance actually works. For many people, this may be a surprise. Modern finance is not so much about traditional financial contracts (stocks, bonds, mortgages, etc.) as about cash flows—the monies arising from these mortgage payments, interest payments, profits, or any other flow of funds. These cash flows can be combined to create all sorts of financial products. The resulting products are often complex, but the underlying process is akin to building with LEGO blocks—with the red and blue pieces assembling the dinosaur replaced by the March and September cash flows constructing the swap.

Arbitrage enters because the cash flows can be structured to create a new or "synthetic" set of financial arrangements, one that retains the desired properties of a traditional contract but achieves it by means of a different structure. Arbitrage does the heavy lifting of making sure these new contracts are priced correctly relative to the original contract. As I make clear in this book, the focus on cash flows and arbitrage brings the power to evaluate not only financial contracts that currently exist but also those contracts that could exist. Modern finance ushered in the age of synthetic securities, and with it the ability to use finance innovatively to make borrowers and lenders alike better-off.

These same innovations, however, also give rise to the ethical challenges I consider in this book.

Some observers might wonder why these problems are arising now. One theory is that banking is simply attracting the "wrong" kind of people—that the easy money available in structuring complex financial products is attracting "bad apples" who see nothing wrong in exploiting other people.[6] Yet, others are less sure, arguing that "ethical problems in organizations originate not with 'a few bad apples' but with the 'barrel makers'"—that is, with the management of the bank, or even with the nature of the financial system more generally.[7] We discuss that issue in chapter 6 in the context of Bank of America's selling bad mortgage loans to unsuspecting buyers, but overall it seems hard to believe that ethical problems in banking are simply due to personnel issues.

Perhaps a more relevant question is what makes financial decision-making prone to overlook ethical dimensions? One reason may be that markets, which play an increasingly important role in the economy, can lead to a diminished sense of social responsibility—that the impersonality of market settings can lead participants to overlook moral consequences that would otherwise deter bad behavior. A growing body of experimental economics research shows that considerations of "fairness," for example, have little effect on market outcomes.[8] Similarly, psychology research suggests that setting out issues in terms of money payoffs rather than nonmoney terms leads to more individualistic behavior.

A particularly intriguing study by the German behavioral researchers Armin Falk and Nora Szech provides troubling evidence of the influence of markets in the context of an experiment in which subjects decide between either saving the life of a mouse or receiving money.[9] The mice in question are used in laboratory experiments, and mice no longer needed for such a purpose (i.e., excess mice) are killed. Individuals were each first presented with a choice: option A, in which the participant receives 10 euros but a mouse is killed, or option B, in which a mouse is spared but the participant forgoes any money. Individuals were then placed in a market setting and randomly assigned to be either a seller (who was given property rights to the mouse) or a buyer. The buyer and seller then bargained in a continuous auction over killing a mouse for a total gain of 20 euros to be split between the two parties, or sparing the mouse for no gain.

The data show a disquieting difference in outcomes between the individual and the market cases. In the individual decision case, 45.9 percent of participants were willing to kill the mouse for 10 euros; in the market setting, 72.2 percent of sellers were willing to do so for prices below or equal to 10 euros. Indeed, to get individuals to kill the mouse at the same high rate as in the market setting required a payment of 47.5 euros. Do experiments with mice necessarily translate into more general settings involving people? Perhaps not, but the evidence here suggests that individuals making decisions in markets seem to put very different weights on moral dimensions than they do in nonmarket settings.

The complexity of modern finance is also part of the problem. What might have been obviously exploitative when contracts were simpler is now concealed by layers of cash flows transformed in ways that require complex calculations even to construct, let alone to value. This makes it harder for the buyer (and sometimes the seller) to understand what is actually being traded. Contributing to this problem is the fact that complex economic activity is now often delegated to agents who act at the behest of principals. For example, the senior banker who interacts with the client is not the financial engineer who actually structures the products being delivered to the client. Complexity can give rise to "indirect agency" problems in which the principal may feel more detached, and so less responsible, for any questionable ethical decisions made in the product design, while the agents may feel that "they are just following orders" and so are also not responsible for considering any ethical dimensions.

Aggravating this tendency are compensation contracts that focus the agent's attention on the completion of specific, narrowly defined tasks. For example, the financial engineer might be asked to "structure a contract that allows our client to bet against the housing market," and he or she is rewarded for successfully completing that contract itself, not on the outcome of the entire project (we discuss that issue when we look at the *SEC v. Goldman Sachs* case in chapter 6). The dispersion of decision-making across individuals can lead to no one's taking responsibility for ethical outcomes.[10]

The impersonality of modern financial markets also obscures the fact that somewhere there is someone on the other side of the trade or deal. Extensive research now demonstrates that the more detached the decision-maker is from the impact of an activity, the less real are the ethical dimensions.[11] Thus, whereas in the "old days" the borrower and lender actually met, these days the borrower may be a homeowner in Las Vegas and the lender an insurance company in Norway, both of whom lack any real details about the other. This impersonality, combined with the transactional nature of many activities in finance, surely works against incentives to build a reputation for fair dealing. It can also work against building a culture of "doing the right thing" within a banking organization.

There is another problem: it is not always obvious what the "right" thing to do actually is. Winners and losers emerge naturally in markets. So when do things cross the line into the exploitative? The complexity and innovation of financial techniques can obscure the big picture for those actually working in the financial markets. It can be equally difficult to discern for those outside the markets, particularly those not conversant in the mechanics of modern finance who may see only "greed" at work and not appreciate when and how finance can actually make everyone better-off.

And so our quest to sort out when the positive effects of finance generate "something for nothing," or when those activities lead to the opposite outcome where financiers take the gains and society pays the cost. To do so, along the way some readers may have to learn about finance, some may have to learn about ethics, and we all have to figure out their intersection—a daunting and certainly ambitious task.

In the next chapter, I explain the role of cash flows in finance, what the concept of arbitrage means, and how removing inefficiencies can make markets better-off but not necessarily every individual within the market. While these fundamentals underlie modern finance, I first show how the medieval *contractus trinus* and its more modern application in Islamic finance, the *murabaha* contract, are based on the same concept—create "new" securities that have the properties you want in a more user-friendly format (in these cases, create securities that essentially pay interest but do not violate religious rules against doing so). I then explain the evolution of modern finance, focusing on three important steps: the concept of "homemade leverage," the option pricing revolution, and the development of swaps. I explain how modern finance allows you to transform the cash flows you have into the cash flows you need for the security that you want. I also discuss why modern finance really is a step forward from the old "boring finance," which seemingly limited the misdeeds of banks and Wall Street firms.

Chapter 3 provides concrete examples of how this cash flow approach of modern finance works. I show how to create mortgage-backed securities, structured loans, and synthetic corporate bonds. These examples illustrate how arbitrage-based strategies work, and why winners and losers emerge as natural by-products. This chapter is more technical, and readers new to finance may find it helpful to skim (or even skip if they are getting lost) and come back to it in the context of the specific examples discussed in later chapters.

We then turn to the ethics side of the equation. In chapter 4, I set out a variety of perspectives on what constitutes ethical behavior in markets. "Sharp dealing" in financial markets has a long history, but there have always been limits suggested by religious, legal, philosophical, and even "folk-based" cultural foundations of right and wrong. I give an overview of these approaches, with the goal of showing why some things can be wrong—i.e., unethical—even if they may not be illegal (thus falling into the "weasel zone" noted earlier).

Yet it can be hard to reconcile these dictums with the realities of markets, and I address this issue in chapter 5. If your job is to maximize shareholder value, why do you—or even can you—care about the person on the other side of a deal? Arbitrage usually results in winners and losers—if markets are for consenting adults, why should you ever care about the loser? Such market puzzles highlight why none of this is straightforward, and why seemingly ethical people can fail to recognize what appears patently obvious to others.

How, then, to determine these ethical boundaries in modern financial markets? Like many before me, I suggest looking to motivation for an answer. If an activity's purpose is to deceive, to cheat others, to exploit complexity to take advantage of others, then it is surely suspect. In the following chapters, I head "into the gray" by looking at concrete examples of market behaviors that fall into these general categories. In chapter 6, I illustrate the problems of deception by looking at Lehman Brothers Repo 105, the flawed mortgage-backed securities issued by Bank of America and its subsidiaries Countrywide Financial and Merrill Lynch, and the Goldman Sachs Abacus deal. These cases illustrate how arbitrage-based strategies can be used to deceive counterparties and the market, behavior that is surely dubious if not altogether illegal.

Arbitrage is often used to exploit rigidities in markets arising in many cases from regulation. In chapter 7, I consider how regulatory arbitrage, though beneficial in principle, can cross the lines of ethical behavior. I provide one (perhaps surprising) example of the positive use of arbitrage—Bernie Madoff and the Cincinnati Stock Exchange—and two less surprising bad examples of arbitrage strategies—JPMorgan Chase and the California energy markets, and Goldman Sachs and the aluminum market. In the JPMorgan case, the question becomes when does arbitrage behavior cross the line from ameliorating market inefficiencies to manipulating markets? In the Goldman case, the focus is on the ethics of commercial transactions—how far can you go in exploiting customers and markets?

In chapter 8, I consider how the complexity arising from arbitrage-based activities can be used to take advantage of other participants and the market. Here I look to issues posed by statistical arbitrage and high-frequency trading (HFT). Many HFT activities are very beneficial to markets, while others, such as quote dangling and spoofing, are clearly illegal. Yet other activities are more nuanced—is setting up an algorithm to take advantage of another algorithm ethical? Are strategies posing large risks to the entire market ever ethically acceptable? When does speed lead to unfair advantages over others in the market? The issues here take gray to a whole new level of charcoal.

Chapter 9 returns to the issue of arbitraging the rules by looking at the incentives of borrowers and lenders. We first look at the intriguing problem of toxic loans in France. These complex financial arrangements exploited accounting rules in Europe to allow municipalities to borrow more cheaply in return for assuming outsize risks via embedded options. The question here is whether it was ethical for the large banks to offer these loans or for the municipalities to take them? This sets the stage for revisiting the issues raised in the beginning of the book of how Goldman Sachs helped Greece get into the eurozone. What exactly did it do? Was Goldman wrong? In light of the current Greek situation, the answer remains timely.

The book's final two chapters step back out of the fog to consider the challenge of arbitrage and ethics for market participants. Religion, law, and philosophy all make it clear that ethical boundaries exist in financial markets. And, as the various examples demonstrate, ethical lapses occur in a wide range of settings. Yet, while it is easy to observe transgressions after the fact, are the boundaries of ethical behavior as obvious when they arise in new or unique circumstances? Can we, in fact, recognize ethical dilemmas when they crop up? Research in behavioral ethics suggests that you will be better able to do so if you are aware of the inherent biases that affect ethical decision-making. In that chapter, I briefly describe these behavioral biases with the goal of suggesting ways to recognize when using financial techniques can cross ethical boundaries.

I also discuss the important role of culture in creating an environment in which ethical decision-making prevails. Firms, particularly financial firms, have struggled with the problem of creating an environment or culture that leads employees to make the "right" choices when facing gray areas. I discuss various approaches being taken to address this problem, both by firms and by regulators. I also argue that the finance profession and finance professors, in particular, have a role to play in creating an ethical culture. In our teaching and research, we have to change from viewing finance as simply a set of tools that can be applied indiscriminately to showing more how we can use financial techniques to make a positive difference in society.

The book's final chapter considers the larger question of the ethical limits of arbitrage, and in particular what can be done to change the current environment of financial scandals. While it is tempting to demand more rules and regulations, I argue that this misses a fundamental feature of modern finance: the more specificity there is, the easier it is to devise replication strategies that can arbitrage around the rules and regulations. This does not mean, however, that finance is unstoppable, that the "weasel zone" is just the natural milieu of modern finance. Instead, I argue that the solution is to shift more to standards-based regulation. As I discuss, this approach turns the conventional wisdom that standards work best when participants are trustworthy, and rules work best when they are not, on its head. Indeed, I maintain that creating a plethora of rules actually *incentivizes* the very behavior it seeks to restrict by creating an environment in which arbitrage-based strategies can flourish. Recognizing this new reality of modern finance can set the stage for regulation to channel the power of finance into positive, and not negative, endeavors.

The current profusion of financial scandals at major financial firms testifies to the importance of solving this problem. So, too, do the woeful data from surveys regarding the perceived ethical standards of financial services firms. For the fourth consecutive year, banks and financial services firms placed dead last in the Edelman global ranking of trust in industries. A recent Harris poll found that 68 percent of those surveyed disagreed with the statement "In general, people on Wall Street are as honest and moral as other people."[12] The Gallup poll on honesty and ethics across different professions is equally sobering—only 28 percent of respondents deemed bankers trustworthy, and that number fell to 11 percent for stockbrokers. Only members of Congress, car salesmen, and telemarketers fared worse.[13]

But to solve the problem we have to understand it, and to that end we turn to the development of modern finance.

CHAPTER 2

THE EVOLUTION OF MODERN FINANCE

MODERN FINANCE GIVES a prominent role to arbitrage. As we discussed in the preceding chapter, the concept of arbitrage involves "buying low and selling high." For those steeped in traditional finance, an arbitrage opportunity arises in the context of a security trading in two places at different prices; buying the security where it is cheaper and selling it where it is more expensive forces prices to the point where a single price is restored across both markets. But arbitrage can also be used in more creative ways, such as working backward to create a "new" set of financial arrangements, one that retains the desired properties of the original contract but achieves it via a different structure—and is priced correctly. Using arbitrage techniques in this way makes it possible both to create new opportunities and to circumvent restrictions that may be limiting market behaviors.

The quintessential example of this use of arbitrage is the *contractus trinus* illustrated in Figure 1. Introduced in the thirteenth century, this technique circumvented the Catholic Church's prohibition against interest-bearing loans by having an investor enter

Figure 1

The Contractus Trinus

(THREEFOLD CONTRACT)

LENDER	BORROWER
The Investment (or Loan)	
Lender "invests" with borrower $x for one year	Borrower gets $x as an investment
The Insurance Contract (to guarantee against default)	
Lender receives insurance from the borrower on the investment	Borrower writes an insurance contract on the investment
The Sale of Profit (the return of x + r)	
Lender sells to the borrower the right to any profit over a pre-specified % of the investment	Borrower pays back x plus the amount below the pre-specified level (r)

The *contractus trinus* was a way to circumvent the Catholic Church's prohibition against charging interest on loans in medieval times. Individually each contract is compliant with the ban on interest, but collectively they create an interest-paying loan.

into three contracts—an investment, an insurance contract, and a sale of profit.[1] While each of these contracts is individually compliant with the ban on usury, in combination they essentially create an interest-bearing loan. Such a multipart approach also underlies the *murabaha* contract, a mainstay of Islamic finance designed as a way around the Koran's proscription of *riba*, or usury (we will revisit this contract in chapter 11).[2] It is not only modern financiers who have understood the benefits of financial engineering!

In modern financial markets, arbitrage-based techniques have found new life; financial scholarship and technology are setting the stage for arbitrage techniques to apply much more broadly. This is because the building blocks of modern finance are not securities themselves or particular financial contracts, but rather the underlying cash flows that they create. Whether these cash flows are in the context of a mortgage payment, a dividend, an interest payment, or an option payoff, the timing and structure of the cash flows are what determine the payoff to the investor. As we will discuss in this chapter, focusing on cash flows and arbitrage brings the power to evaluate not only financial contracts that currently exist but also those contracts that could exist. Modern finance ushered in the age of synthetic securities and, with it, some of the ethical challenges we consider in this book.

Modern Finance—First Steps

To understand this evolution, we will take a quick journey through three major milestones in finance. These milestones—the home-made leverage concept of Modigliani and Miller (MM), the option pricing revolution, and the development of swaps—took finance from the world of stocks, bonds, and bank loans to a world of structured cash flows having whatever properties the holder needs and wants.

We begin with what is generally viewed as the dawn of modern finance, the Modigliani-Miller theorems. Franco Modigliani and Merton Miller were economists (and later Nobel laureates) who crafted their eponymous theorems while working on the faculty of Carnegie-Mellon University. Modigliani and Miller looked at a basic question in finance: is there an optimal capital structure for a firm?[3] Capital structure refers to the debt and equity a firm uses to finance its operations. Some firms, such as Facebook, have little debt, relying instead on selling stock or using the retained profits not distributed in dividends or buy backs to finance the firm. Other firms are highly leveraged, issuing bonds, or borrowing via bank loans or other debt to augment small amounts of capital to fund operations. Having only a small amount of equity in the capital structure magnifies the gains (and losses) to the owners, but it also exposes the firm to a greater risk of bankruptcy because creditors have to be paid before the equity holders. Thus, every firm has to address the question of its optimal mix of debt and equity.

Modigliani and Miller's seminal paper in 1958 provided a surprising answer: there is no optimal capital structure, since the mix of debt and equity does not matter. In a world with no taxes or other frictions, a firm's value is independent of its capital structure.[4] Consequently, with the firm indifferent to capital structures, so, too, should be its shareholders. The reason why this is true is a concept MM called "homemade leverage." MM argued that the market value of any firm depended upon its role in an investor's overall portfolio. Suppose, for example, that an investor holds only a particular firm's stock and that firm has zero leverage (i.e., that firm has no debt). If the investor prefers a more levered position (yielding greater returns but, of course, more risk), then he or she could buy the stock by borrowing funds at the personal level, effectively creating a portfolio at the personal level that replicates a more levered stock position at the firm level. Conversely, an investor could offset too large a levered position at the firm level by holding greater amounts of risk-free assets along with the stock. With the investors able to create the risk profile they desire, there is no optimal capital structure at the firm level.

This result provoked many objections, most of which focused on real-world imperfections assumed away in the MM analysis. In particular, an important feature of the "real world" is that for the firm debt is tax deductible, whereas equity is not. This disparity suggested that debt could be more valuable to the firm than equity, undermining the notion that the firm should be indifferent to its capital structure. On the other hand, bankruptcy is a very costly event for a firm, and bankruptcy costs were also not considered in the friction-free world of MM (1958). Because greater equity can forestall bankruptcy, equity could have greater value to the firm, again challenging MM's irrelevance argument.

In subsequent work, MM (and a multitude of later finance researchers) clarified these effects, showing that there were various influences on a firm's optimal capital structure. From the investor's perspective, however, the firm's decisions became secondary: the investors can structure the exposure they want by leveraging or deleveraging on their own. This shifted the focus of finance from the cash flows the firm provided to the portfolio of cash flows the investor desired.

The Option Pricing Revolution

This collection of cash flow concepts also underlies a cornerstone of modern finance—option pricing theory. It may seem odd that option pricing plays such a pivotal role, particularly given that options per se have been around for centuries, and that other categories of financial assets (stocks and bonds, for example) are far more prevalent. Indeed, the complexity of options had long hindered their trading in markets in large part because of the difficulty of valuing them.[5] Research by Fisher Black, Myron Scholes, and Robert Merton would overcome this difficulty and provide a new framework for valuing "contingent claims" (the generic name given to options and other derivative securities).

The key to this framework is recognizing that an option's value can be understood only in relation to the value of other financial instruments. This concept, known as "relative pricing," relies on the notion that in an efficient market arbitrage brings the prices of equivalent cash flows into alignment. A particularly important special case of this concept is known as "put-call parity." To understand what this is and how it works, let us start with what we mean by a put and a call. A call option gives the holder the right to buy a particular stock at a given price (called the strike price), while a put option gives the holder the right to sell the stock at a given strike price. An option contract lasts for a specified time period, and in return for this right to buy or sell the holder pays the writer a fee, or option premium.[6]

That the put, the call, and the stock price must all somehow align was recognized long ago. Leonard Higgins, writing in 1896, observed that "a put can be turned into a call by buying all the stock" and "a call can be turned into a put by selling all the stock."[7] A more formal way to express these interrelationships is the put-call parity formula:

$$C = P + S - BK$$

In this equation, C and P are current prices of a call option and a put option that each have strike price K and expiration t, B is the current price of a zero-coupon bond that pays a dollar at time t, and S is the current price of the underlying stock. This equation shows that a call option should have the same value as buying the stock with borrowed money (this is what the S – BK term captures; it is essentially buying the stock on margin) and then insuring the value of the stock with a put option (the P term). This relationship means we have two ways to have a call option: the natural call option, C, on the left hand side of the equation, and the synthetic call option created on the right hand side of the equation.[8]

For our purposes, it is important to recognize that arbitrage will keep this relationship intact. If buying the natural call is more expensive in the market than constructing its synthetic counterpart, then arbitrageurs will sell the natural call and buy the synthetic call; if the natural call is less expensive, then the opposite transaction will occur. In valuing these contracts what matters are the underlying cash flows; in modern finance, arbitrage will do the heavy lifting of making sure that like cash flows are priced the same.

The concept of put-call parity is both useful and powerful, but it is also limited. Because the stock price moves over the duration of the option contract, the exact value of the option may be difficult to determine. What is needed is a model that can give exact solutions for the option price, and starting with the work of Louis Bachelier, in 1900, legions of researchers worked on exactly that problem.[9] But there was always a stumbling block: if the option depended on the stock, wouldn't its value also depend upon the expected return to the stock over the time of the option contract?[10] And, as anyone who has ever watched CNBC can attest, there is rarely agreement on what this expected return should be.

The breakthrough in option pricing came with the development of the Black-Scholes model (and related work by Robert Merton). The mathematics behind the Black-Scholes model is complex (and reviewing the stochastic calculus needed to solve the model would take us far afield from our objective). But the underlying notions can be captured by a fairly intuitive argument that constructs a "perfect hedge." With the perfect hedge in place, the option price is determined by its relation to a set of observable variables.

To understand this approach, I draw on arguments set out cogently by my colleagues Robert Jarrow and Arka Chatterjea.[11] Let us first note that the call price and the stock price have to move together, reflecting that as the stock price goes up the right to buy the stock at the fixed strike price (the call) also becomes more valuable. Suppose now that you were to hold a "short" position in the stock (i.e., you borrow the stock, sell it, and plan to repurchase the stock at a later date when you have to return the borrowed stock). You will make money on a short position if the stock price falls, and you will lose money if the stock price rises. Thus, the short stock position and the call should move in *opposite* directions when the stock price moves. For example, when the stock price goes down, the call is less valuable but the short position in the stock is more valuable. While moving in opposite directions, however, the call and the short stock position may not be moving by exactly the same amount. So the final step is to balance our position by selling a fraction of each share of stock for each call we hold. This fraction is the hedge ratio, and it adjusts our position to create a perfect hedge.[12] Now, no matter what happens to the stock price, the call value and the value of the short stock position will be perfectly aligned to keep the value of the overall position the same. To avoid arbitrage, this perfectly hedged position must earn the risk-free rate.

This hedging argument underlies the Black-Scholes formula, which shows that an option price depends upon the stock price, the strike price, the time to maturity, the risk-free interest rate, and volatility of the underlying stock return. What it does not depend upon are expectations of the stock's future return. Thus, the problem that had thwarted earlier attempts to price the option was circumvented, opening the door to pricing complex derivatives. Now, by creating a synthetic position that exactly captured the change in the option value, we could determine the option price. And, as before, arbitrage would keep these natural and synthetic prices in line.

So, building from MM's insight that homemade leverage could allow an investor to create a set of cash flows different from what a particular security supplied, the option pricing model now provided a way to price those cash flows. And once you could do this, a natural question arose: could you transform the cash flows you have into the cash flows you need for the security you want? While this next step sounds complicated, the process is greatly facilitated by a third important step in the evolution of modern finance—swaps.

Swaps

Swaps are contractual agreements between two parties to exchange one set of cash flows for another. As we will discuss, swaps can involve a wide range of cash flows, but the earliest and perhaps most widely used financial swap products involve interest rates. Interest rate swaps are financial contracts in which the parties agree to swap a fixed payment for a floating payment over the life of the swap. The party that buys the swap pays the fixed rate, and the party that sells the swap pays the floating rate. The swap itself does not involve any actual borrowing or lending, but it is based on a notional principle amount (for example, $1 million). As we will see, adding a swap to an existing position can transform the security you have into the security you want.

To explain the concept, suppose both you and your neighbor took out thirty-year mortgages for $300,000 but yours was for a fixed-rate mortgage and his was for a variable-rate mortgage. If now you both wished you had done the opposite (why didn't I borrow variable? Or what an idiot—why didn't I take out the fixed rate loan?), you could in principle accomplish the same thing by simply agreeing to swap payments; you send your neighbor the payment for his variable mortgage, he sends you the payment for your fixed mortgage, and you both then pay what you owe to your respective lenders. In effect, you have both added another contract to your existing mortgages (the mortgage + the swap), thereby creating a new synthetic position. Adding a pay-variable position to a fixed-rate mortgage creates a synthetic variable-rate mortgage; adding a pay-fixed position to a variable-rate mortgage creates a synthetic fixed-rate mortgage.

If interest rates stay the same, you neither gain nor lose. But if interest rates go up, the person now paying the variable rate has to pay more; whereas if interest rates go down, the person swapping to pay the fixed rate loses out on what would have been a lower interest rate. A swap is a "zero-sum game," so what one person loses the other person gains.

In reality, people do not generally swap mortgage payments, but there are many types of swaps used extensively in actual markets. For example, a "plain vanilla" three-year swap is priced off of the three-year U.S. Treasury bond rate, and swap payments are made every six months (i.e., a three-year swap will have six payment dates). So, ignoring transactions costs, the buyer of the swap agrees to pay a fixed cash flow equal to the three-year Treasury bond rate plus some spread as of the start of the swap and receive a variable cash flow equal to the LIBOR rate (the London Interbank Offered Rate) in force at the time of each payment. The seller agrees to pay the variable LIBOR rate in force at the time of each payment and receive the fixed cash payment. The LIBOR rate is a "floating" rate, meaning that the actual rate the seller pays will vary over the life of the swap. These cash flows, which will take place every six months for the three-year swap period, are illustrated in Figure 2.

Why might someone want to do this? Again, we need to look at the overall position that each participant has. Suppose that a firm has a variable-rate bank loan and is concerned that interest rates might go up and cause it to have to pay more on the loan.

Figure 2

An Interest Rate Swap

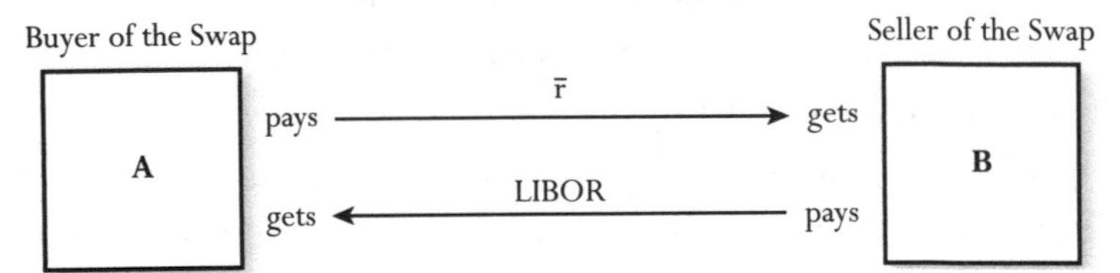

In an interest rate swap, the buyer pays the fixed rate $\bar{r}$ and gets the variable rate LIBOR (the London Interbank Offer Rate). The seller pays the variable rate and gets the fixed rate. The fixed rate is set at the beginning of the swap, while the variable rate will change over the life of the swap. Payments are made at prespecified times during the life of the swap.

Creating a position containing a pay-fixed swap and a variable-rate bank loan effectively creates a synthetic fixed-rate bank loan. Alternatively, a corporate treasurer may have issued fixed-rate bonds and now wishes to take advantage of what may be a lower interest rate environment. A call provision allowing the firm to buy back the bonds at a given price is very expensive, however, so another way to do that is to add a pay-variable swap to a fixed rate bond, thereby creating a synthetic variable rate bond.

These synthetic positions mirror the cash flows of the natural positions, but there is one difference: the synthetic positions have an added counterparty risk because the person (or more accurately, the bank) on the other side of the swap might default. This risk is generally very small, and it manifests itself in a small premium built into the swap. What matters for our purposes is that using swaps allows you to transform cash flows. While we have looked at transforming variable-rate into fixed-rate flows (and vice versa), the process goes far beyond interest rates. Euro-denominated cash flows can be turned into dollar-denominated cash flows via currency swaps. Exposures to bond returns can be turned into exposures to stock returns via total rate of return swaps. Barrels of oil can be turned into dollar-based cash flows via commodity swaps. Swaps can be used to transform virtually any type of cash flows.

In this fashion, they have contributed to the transformation of finance. Starting with Modigliani and Miller's insight regarding homemade leverage, finance moved forward to create synthetically the cash flows you want rather than simply the cash flows you have. And once you can price those cash flows, you can create a vast array of financial products, setting the stage for the development of synthetic securities. The age of modern finance had begun.

Arbitrage Revisited

Lest we get ahead of ourselves and create legions of synthetic products, we should revisit the concept of arbitrage and the starring role it plays in modern finance. Arbitrage removes inefficiencies in markets. Inefficiencies arise for all sorts of reasons, including transactions costs, rigidities in prices, market structure rules, taxes, informational problems—the list goes on and on. Whatever the cause, inefficiencies can result in different prices for like things—what economists call a violation of the "law of one price." Arbitraging those differences away can bring prices, and markets, back into alignment.

Simple arbitrage involves buying where it is cheap and selling where it is expensive. A classic example is gold trading in New York and London. Suppose the gold price is lower in London than in New York. If the price difference is large enough, it makes sense to buy the gold in London, ship it to New York, and then sell it at the higher NY price. These transactions will induce changes in both markets—the higher demand in London to buy gold will push up the price there and the corresponding increase in the supply of gold in New York will force prices down there. When will it stop? Once the prices adjusted for the cost of transporting the gold are equal in the two markets, arbitrage opportunities cease. So an important point to note is that arbitrage does not require prices to be exactly the same; rather, it must be that prices are equilibrated after incorporating the transactions costs of doing so.

Arbitrage is a ubiquitous activity in financial markets. Crude oil, for instance, can be broken down into components of gasoline and heating oil. So if the price of the crude oil futures contract is out of line with the price of the gasoline futures contract and the heating oil futures contracts (taking account of the conversion costs), then arbitrageurs will sell the expensive contract(s) and buy the cheaper one(s). Similarly, if a Canadian stock is cross-listed and trades in both Toronto and New York, then its prices in the two markets can diverge. Of course, this divergence is a bit tricky because the stock is priced in Canadian dollars in Toronto and in U.S. dollars in New York, but given the exchange rate, if the Canadian price is too low the arbitrage is to sell the stock in New York, convert the proceeds into Canadian dollars, and buy the stock in Canada. Market makers also routinely arbitrage across related securities. Given the option pricing model, if the March Ford $14 call option is mispriced relative to the June Ford $14 call option, the market maker will sell the overpriced call and buy the underpriced call. Making markets efficient can be a profitable activity.

Regardless of the setting, arbitrage also makes markets better because, with prices aligned, resources can be allocated to their most efficient uses. Making the market better, however, does not necessarily make each individual in the market better-off. The person who sold the gold cheaply in London would have been better-off selling once the price had been restored to the higher equilibrium value. But such is life—the seller freely chose to sell in London rather than performing the complex arbitrage described above. Perhaps for this seller the transactions costs of putting the arbitrage together exceeded the benefits from doing so. The arbitrageur's gain is often someone else's loss.

Arbitrage also need not be risk-free. If you can instantaneously enter both sides of the trade, then the arbitrageur can lock in a risk-less profit by buying at the low price and selling at the high price, all the while having no capital actually tied up in the position. This is the "classic" arbitrage typically referred to by economists, and it is the reason why arbitrage is sometimes referred to as creating "something from nothing." But there are also risky variants of arbitrage. Hedge funds, for example, often engage in statistical arbitrage (or "stat arb"). Suppose that two securities' prices are highly correlated, so that when one security's price goes up the other's generally does the same. For example, Halliburton Company (ticker symbol HAL) and Helmerich & Payne, Inc. (ticker HP) are both in the energy business, and they have a daily average correlation over the past year of 96.9 percent.[13] If HAL's price ticks up, then the arbitrageur should sell the first security and buy the second—in effect selling high and buying low. Of course, the price of HP may not actually go up, but the arbitrageur is relying on the fact that it is statistically very likely to do so to make profits on average. This type of statistical arbitrage, albeit with correlations measured over a much shorter interval, is also used extensively by high-frequency traders, an issue we will discuss in chapter 8.

Arbitrage is a powerful tool. It can tie markets together and force prices to efficient levels, all the while providing profits to arbitrageurs. Whether it involves gold, heating oil, options, or Canadian securities, the process of arbitrage is essentially the same: buy low and sell high. And, extended to the cash flow level, it is this process that allows for synthetic securities to be priced and traded.

Finance Revisited

In the next chapter, we take up the creation of these new financial products, but before turning to the "how" it may be useful to consider the "why." Specifically, why is modern finance a step forward from the old ways of traditional contracts in which banking was "boring" but at least not seemingly lethal? Are we really any better-off with these new complex financial products than we were with those simpler financial arrangements?

I think nostalgia for the simplicity of times past misses the many ways in which financial markets were both restrictive and deficient. My own experience in buying my first house in upstate New York provides a case in point. At that time, New York State had usury ceilings, so banks could offer mortgage loans only below a specified interest rate. Unfortunately, market interest rates were well above that level, so no bank was actually making new mortgage loans, and prospective home buyers either had to find a seller with an "assumable mortgage" (and a willingness to take on a note for the rest of the needed financing) or qualify for a federal program (such as FHA or VA) that was exempt from such ceilings. Being relatively low-paid fledgling university professors, we fit into the latter category, but doing so greatly limited the house price we could pay because FHA mortgages had a maximum loan size. Thus, buyers and sellers alike were trapped by a system that was "safe" and intended to be "fair" but was actually dysfunctional.

To me, the answer to the "why" question is apparent: modern financial products can better meet the needs of both individuals and the economy. A prospective home buyer in Arizona can get a mortgage because a securitized mortgage product sold to an insurance company in Sweden provides the funding for the loan. A union pension fund in Texas can better meet its obligations because it can buy a "tranche" (or piece) of a structured financial product whose returns are tailored to its specific maturity and risk needs. A solar energy entrepreneur can get needed funds because a securitized offering provides access to a new group of investors—who, in turn, also benefit from getting access to a new investment opportunity. The potential for modern finance to make markets, people, and the economy better-off is a compelling reason to get it right.

CHAPTER 3

ARBITRAGE IN ACTION

> But I dream things that never were;
> and I ask why not?
>
> —G. B. SHAW,
> *Back to Methuselah*, PART I, SCENE I

GEORGE BERNARD SHAW was not speaking about finance when he penned those words, but they capture well why modern finance has had such an impact on financial markets. Equipped with the tools of modern finance, it is a very small step from trading the financial products that you have to creating the financial products that you want. The formula is straightforward: use the underlying cash flows to create an alternative, correctly priced security that has the properties that you want.

The creation of securities can be relatively straightforward as in a mortgage-backed security (MBS), more complicated as in a collateralized debt obligation (CDO), or extremely complex as in a synthetic CDO. To illustrate the process of turning cash flows into securities, we will in this section look at three general examples: mortgage-backed securities, structured loans, and synthetic corporate bonds. Later in the book, we will encounter more complex variants of the process when we turn to particular uses (and misuses) of arbitrage-based techniques and more specialized structured products.*

Putting the Cash Flows to Work

Mortgage-Backed Securities

Consider, for example, the creating of a basic fixed-rate MBS. To do so, a financial firm, say Deutsche Bank, buys up underlying fixed-rate mortgages from firms (typically banks or mortgage brokers) that specialize in originating mortgages. Each underlying mortgage is then placed together with many similar mortgages to form a collection, or pool, of mortgages. These underlying mortgages (which will be known as the collateral) provide a stream of monthly cash flows because the mortgage holders will be making their monthly payments, as they are required to do. The issuer of the MBS then issues new securities based on the cash flows of the underlying collateral (the mortgages). These new securities can all be the same (as in a Ginnie Mae security), or there can be multiple pieces, or "tranches" (e.g., an A tranche, a B tranche, and a C tranche), giving the holders different claims on the underlying cash flows. These new securities are then sold to investors. The structures are illustrated in Figure 3.

Although the cash flows connected with a fixed-rate mort-

---

* Since all this gets a bit technical, readers new to the subject who are finding it hard to navigate may do well to skim this chapter and then come back to it as needed when we look at specific examples involving such financial products in subsequent chapters.

gage seem pretty straightforward (i.e., the mortgage holder sends in a fixed payment each month for the life of the mortgage), the cash flows of the pool of mortgages are a bit more complicated. Credit risk is not usually a problem, because the main MBS issu-

Figure 3
Mortgage-Backed Securities

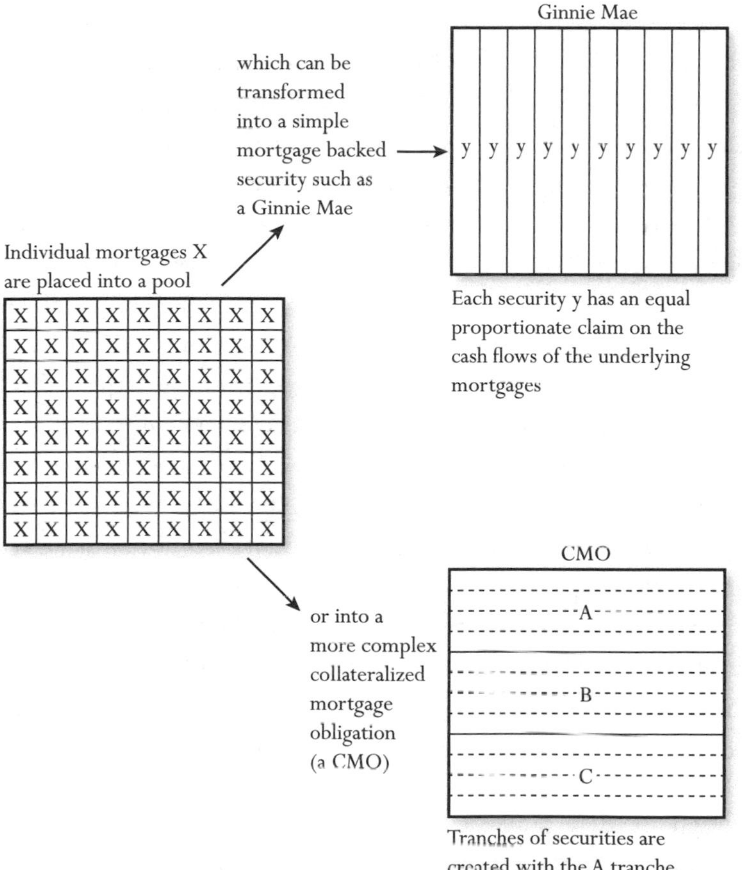

ers (Fannie Mae, Freddie Mac, and Ginnie Mae) insure the MBS against default. But the exact timing and duration of the cash flows is uncertain because the underlying mortgages actually contain an imbedded option. In particular, the borrower can always decide to pay off the mortgage by sending in a check for the remaining balance. In finance parlance, he or she has a call option on the mortgage (or the right to buy it back) with the strike price equal to the outstanding balance. When people refinance their mortgage or sell their house, the remaining principle on that original mortgage loan flows into the pool and is distributed to the MBS holders.

This prepayment risk can be a problem for the holders of the mortgage-backed securities. People generally refinance when mortgage rates have fallen, so the holders of the MBS get back money that they will have to reinvest somewhere else at the now lower interest rates. But even if rates haven't fallen, prepayment shortens the maturity of the MBS holders' investment. For example, if you purchased an MBS with a 5 percent yield and an expected life of nine years, increased prepayments may shorten the expected life of the MBS to five years. Of course, the flows of principal into the pool can also go in the opposite direction, or what is called extension risk. If the economy cools off, or interest rates go up, fewer people may pay off their mortgages early, causing the MBS to last longer than expected.

The uncertainty of the timing of the cash flows is a major risk for the MBS holder, and so it should be priced in the security's yield. To see how, let's return to the notion that the MBS is actually a composite security. When it is guaranteed against default risk, the MBS can be viewed like a government bond in that it gives the holder a guaranteed stream of cash flows in the future (this is also known as an annuity). Because of the imbedded option in the mortgages, the MBS also contains a short position on a call option on that annuity (i.e., the investors in the mortgages have written the call option that the underlying mortgage borrowers can choose to exercise). So the MBS can be considered equal to an annuity plus a short call option.

The value of the call option will increase with volatility (recall the option pricing discussion earlier). The yield on the MBS should thus be close to the yield on a government-guaranteed bond of a similar expected maturity plus a spread that varies positively with volatility. Greater volatility makes the underlying option to prepay more valuable and would be expected to lead to increased prepayments, a shorter MBS maturity, and a fall in the value of the MBS. Lower volatility makes the option to prepay less valuable and should lead to less prepayment, a longer MBS life, and an increase in the value of the MBS.

Thus, building from the cash flows of the underlying mortgages, the holder of the MBS now has a fixed-income security with a government-based guarantee against default that trades at a premium to a Treasury security. In a standard MBS like a Ginnie Mae, the holders share equally in these cash flows, so that the timing of the cash flow stream, and exactly how long the security will last, is a risk borne by each holder. Alternatively, an MBS can be structured to provide partial protection against this timing uncertainty by means of a tranche structure. The tranche structure "passes through" the cash flows in a sequential manner, with the A tranche receiving the first principal payments (both scheduled and prepayments), and then once the A is fully paid out, on to the B tranche, to the C tranche, etc. This tranche-structured MBS is generally known as a CMO (collateralized mortgage obligation).

Whereas in the standard MBS, each holder receives the same yield, the yields in the CMO will differ across tranches. This is because by sequencing the cash flows the securitization process essentially creates a series of securities, each with a different expected set of temporal cash flows. Since the A tranche gets all of the first payments, its expected life is fairly short, often on the order of two years or less. Consequently, its yield should compare to that of a short-term government bond, and the additional option-based spread should be smaller owing to the already compressed nature of the cash flows. The subsequent tranches (the B, C, D, . . . , even possibly a Z tranche that mimics a zero-coupon bond) will have yields that track their expected maturities, influenced as well by the effects of the expected prepayment speed.

Using the CMO structure, the underlying cash flows have morphed into a portfolio of securities that can be sold to a variety of borrowers who might otherwise never invest in a mortgage-based product. For example, an investor looking for a safe short-term fixed-income investment may be tempted by the A tranche security, while a life insurer looking for a long-term asset may find the Z tranche an attractive investment. Securitizing the cash flows brings new options for investors and new funding sources for borrowers—benefits made possible by the development of modern finance.

A Structured Loan

The preceding example involved rearranging the cash flows to create different securities. As we saw earlier, however, cash flows can also be transformed by the simple addition of another contract to an existing contract (recall that a fixed-rate mortgage plus a swap became a synthetic variable-rate mortgage). A structured loan is a bank loan that includes an embedded option. Structured loans are used by borrowers who want to change (and potentially lower) the cost and timing of loan repayments. As we will see in chapter 9, these products can be very complex (and much abused), but they can allow borrowers to change the cash flows that they owe into a payment stream that they prefer. In what follows, we consider a simple example of a so-called barrier product.[1]

Suppose that a borrower could obtain a three-year loan at the standard current LIBOR rate (recall that the London Interbank Offered Rate is a variable rate and therefore changes over the life of the loan). The borrower would like to get a lower overall funding cost, and to that end the banker suggests adding to the loan another contract—a "short" put option on the LIBOR rate with a strike of, say, 4 percent. From the preceding chapter we know that an option writer (i.e., the "short" position) receives a payment (the "premium") up front but could owe additional amounts to the option holder (the bank) if the option ends up in the money. A put option will be in the money if the LIBOR rate goes below the strike, so the writer of the put benefits if rates stay at or above this level.

Figure 4 gives an example of how this loan plus put option strategy can lower the borrower's cost. Here the put has a strike price of 4 percent, meaning that as long as the LIBOR rate is at or above 4 percent the option expires worthless, but the option writer (the borrower) is paid the option premium. If the LIBOR rate falls below 4 percent, the borrowers' cost remains at 4 percent because their gain from the lower interest rate is offset by the payment they have to make to the holder of the put option (the bank). In effect, adding a short put option to a variable-rate loan gives the lender a "floor" on the loan's interest rate. If the borrower believes rates are unlikely to fall, then this structured loan contract lowers her or his borrowing cost relative to a standard loan contract.

It is easy to see that a wide range of payoff structures is possible by the adding of different option positions to the loan. For example, if the borrower adds to his loan a call option (i.e., takes the "long" position), then this will create a "cap" on his interest rate because when interest rates go up, the gains from the option payoff offset his higher borrowing costs. Adding both the long call and the short put can create a "collar" in which the interest rate is bounded above and below. With the tools of modern finance, structured products can be used to change the required

Figure 4

A Structured Loan

CONTRACTS	PAYMENTS
1. Standard Loan	LIBOR
+	+
2. Sale of a Put Option with 4% Strike	{ -x basis points if LIBOR > 4% 4% - LIBOR otherwise
equals	
3. Structured Loan	{ LIBOR – x basis points if LIBOR > 4% 4% otherwise

A structured loan is a standard bank loan with an embedded option. In this example, the structured loan includes an embedded put option with a strike price of 4 percent. When LIBOR is above 4 percent the option is out of the money, and the option writer gets an option premium of x basis points. If LIBOR is below 4 percent, the option is in the money, and the option writer must pay the difference. This example is similar to those in Christophe Pérignon and Boris Vallée, "The Political Economy of Financial Innovation: Evidence from Local Governments," Working Paper HEC Paris, available at www.bostonfed.org/economic/conf/municipal-finance-2015/papers/vallee.pdf.

cash flows of the loan into a cash flow stream that better meets the needs of the borrower.

Synthetic Corporate Bonds

Another mechanism for turning the cash flows you have into the securities you want involves the process of synthetic asset replication. Suppose you are a pension fund or retirement provider, and you would like to hold only very safe assets such as AAA-rated corporate bonds in your portfolio. Back in 1980, there were sixty U.S. corporations rated triple A by Standard & Poors, but today there are only two such corporations (Johnson & Johnson and Microsoft). Not surprisingly, there are simply not enough AAA bonds in existence to meet the investor demand.

Using the techniques of modern finance, however, you can synthetically create more. To see how this is done, we have to introduce another new instrument in the finance tool box, the credit default swap (CDS). A CDS is not actually a swap, but instead is a type of put option (whoever named it a swap has a lot to answer for). Credit default swaps are contracts in which the seller agrees to provide a payment to the buyer in case of a credit event (the name given to a default or possibly a downgrade) in an underlying security. In return for this protection, the buyer of the CDS pays the seller a fee. Much as in our previous structured loan example, if over the given year there is no credit event, the seller has received a fee but does not have to make any payment. Thus, a CDS is like an insurance contract that pays off when a specified credit event occurs.

CDSs are typically written on an underlying bond or bond index. A holder of a Ford Motor Company 6.5 percent 2018 Bond, for example, could buy a CDS that protects him or her from a default or credit event on that bond. Should Ford default or be downgraded, the CDS provides a payment, effectively protecting the bondholder from credit risk. This insurance feature is a benefit both to the bond buyer and to the overall financial market. Being able to "insure" the bond against credit risk can allow investors who might view bonds as too risky to now invest in the bond. Expanding the universe of potential investors, in turn, can lower the cost to the firm of issuing the bond.

Of course, the CDS can also be used to take on the credit exposure of the bond. In particular, the writer of the CDS is taking on the credit risk and in return receives a yearly premium. If the writer places that premium in a risk-free interest-bearing account, then the cash flows of that overall position essentially replicate the yields of the natural bond.

Figure 5

Natural Bonds and Synthetic Bonds

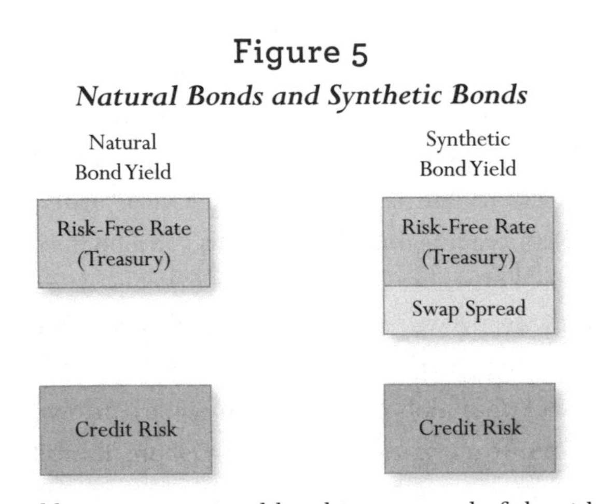

The yield on a conventional bond is composed of the risk-free rate and compensation for the credit risk. One forms the synthetic bond by selling a credit default swap, and then investing the cash inflow from the premium received in a risk-free account. The synthetic bond yield should also depend on the risk-free rate, the credit risk, and a compensation for counterparty risk.

To see how this works, consider the cash flows of the bond and the synthetic bond. If there is no default, the bondholder each year receives the specified coupon on the bond, while the synthetic bond holder receives the premium. If there is a default, the bondholder suffers a loss and so does the holder of the synthetic bond. For these bonds to be substitutes, the yields on both positions must be approximately equal. As Figure 5 shows, the yield to the bond investor can be decomposed into the risk-free yield on a Treasury of similar maturity and an additional yield based on the firm's credit risk. A synthetic bond has the same risk-free yield plus the same credit yield plus a small yield to compensate for the counterparty risk of the CDS. Thus, the synthetic bond yield has to be slightly higher to compensate for this additional risk.

Now consider the role played by arbitrage. If the yield on the natural bond is higher than the yield on the synthetic bond (adjusted for the small risk differential), then arbitrageurs will buy the natural bond and sell the synthetic bond. This drives the price of the natural bond up (and its yield down), while lowering the price of the CDS (and raising its yield). If the yield on the natural bond is lower than the equilibrium yield on the synthetic bond, then arbitrageurs will sell the natural bond and buy the synthetic bond. This process means that the constraints imposed by the natural supply of the bond are now relaxed: if you want more IBM bonds, you simply make more synthetically!

For some readers, the ability for someone other than IBM to create an ersatz IBM bond may be surprising (and a bit unsettling). Such things happen routinely in markets, however, particularly as they relate to derivative contracts. Options contracts, for example, are not created by the company but are offered instead by options markets. A Ford March 14 call is based on the behavior of Ford stock, but it is not an obligation of the Ford

Motor Company. The option is valuable because of the protection or opportunities it provides the option holder given price movements in the underlying stock price. Similarly, what is being created in the synthetic bond is the same *credit exposure* as in the IBM bond. Hence, just as the buyers and sellers of pork belly futures rarely actually want to take delivery of an actual pork belly and instead opt for cash settlement, so here the buyers and sellers of the synthetic bond are more interested in the cash flows of the underlying bond, and not actually in owning the bond per se.[2]

Asset replication techniques that use credit default swaps can be applied to a wide range of cash flows, enabling the creation of all sorts of synthetic securities, such as synthetic sovereign bonds, synthetic mortgage-backed securities, and synthetic index replications. Not surprisingly, these replications can be quite complex, setting the stage for some of the ethical issues we will discuss in later chapters.

Outcomes Revisited

The techniques of modern finance provide a way to transform cash flows in useful ways. It is important to recognize, however, that in the process the risks associated with those cash flows may also be transformed. In some cases, the risks are easy to follow. Participants in an interest rate swap, for example, know that if interest rates go up, one side does better and one side does worse. Swaps are a zero-sum game, so what one side wins the other side loses. Other types of contracts, however, need not have symmetric gains and losses. A CDS, or any option for that matter, is not zero-sum—the option writer gets paid no matter what, and if the option expires worthless, then the option buyer gets nothing.

This does not necessarily mean, though, that the option holder loses. Because contracts are often combined to form composite positions, knowing your gains or losses on one piece of a position does not necessarily indicate your overall gains and losses. As we have seen in this chapter, modern finance involves more of a LEGO approach where financial positions are built up cash flow by cash flow. This can result in complex, nonlinear payoffs that defy easy calculation—at least by some parties in a transaction. Such complexity opens the door to a wide range of questionable practices.

A case in point is the sorry tale of Gibson Greeting Cards (GG) versus Bankers Trust (BT).[3] In 1994 Gibson Greetings sued Bankers Trust, a large U.S. investment bank, claiming "that the bank had sold them high risk, leveraged derivatives without giving them adequate warning of the potential pitfalls."[4] GG and BT had actually entered a series of swaps starting in 1991. The specific swap contracts were often quite complex. For example, one swap specified that Gibson Greetings receive a fixed-rate payment of 5.5 percent and in return make a payment to Bankers Trust equal to the LIBOR rate squared divided by 6 percent. Why anyone, let alone a greeting card company, would enter such a swap is hard to fathom, particularly when one realizes that the outcomes here were heavily skewed in BT's favor. As Jonathan Macey explains in his book *The Death of Corporate Reputation*, if the LIBOR rate is 5.75 percent, the net payments to and from both sides are equal. If rates went down by 300 basis points, Gibson would receive the fixed 5.5 percent but have to pay BT only 1.26 percent, giving Gibson a gain of 4.24 percent. However, if rates went up by 300 basis points, Gibson would receive the 5.5 percent and owe BT 12.76 percent—a loss of 7.25 percent.[5] Over time, Gibson entered into even more complex arrangements with BT, ultimately losing $23 million.

Should Gibson have understood the risks and payoffs before

entering such a contract? Of course, but it argued that it had been intentionally misled by BT with respect to the payoff structure. More intriguing is that Gibson claimed that BT took advantage of "an unknowing customer" to profit at its expense.[6] BT settled the civil case in 1995 without admitting any wrongdoing.[7] BT also signed consent decrees with federal securities regulators and agreed to pay a $10 million fine, all without admitting or denying guilt.

A similar case at about the same time involving swaps written by Bankers Trust with Proctor & Gamble actually did go to trial. The legal issues there focused on the question of whether BT owed P&G fiduciary duties, in which case BT would have owed obligations of duty and care to P&G, a role that went far beyond simply being its counterparty in the trades. There also were allegations that BT had misled P&G on the valuation of swaps it had sold to P&G. The court ultimately ruled in favor of BT with respect to the legal issues, but the market ruled in favor of P&G—firms increasingly turned away from dealing with BT. Decreasing revenues forced BT into a sale to Deutsche Bank in December 1998.

The Gibson Greeting Cards and Proctor & Gamble cases illustrate an important point: what is considered legal and what is considered ethical may not be the same thing. They also highlight that the ethical dimension cannot be overlooked, because trust is always a fundamental component in any financial transaction. How, then, to sort out these ethical lines in a complex financial world? In the next chapter, we turn to this important question.

CHAPTER 4

ETHICS AND FINANCE

Relativity applies to physics, not ethics.

—ALBERT EINSTEIN

WHEN IS SOMETHING "wrong" in markets? Sharp dealing in financial markets has a long, and often inglorious, history. Financial shenanigans range from selling "blue sky" to unwary investors, to running bucket shops selling penny stocks to the naïve, to creating Ponzi schemes or financial pyramids. Some behavior, such as cheating widows and orphans, has always been viewed as wrong. Whether other behaviors cross ethical lines is less clear—knowing more than your counterparty is not a crime, nor is being an astute investor evidence of any ethical failure. Moreover, the lines defining acceptable behavior often seem to shift over time. The activities that made the Jay Goulds (or even the Joseph Kennedys) titans of the market would nowadays run afoul of modern securities laws.

In this chapter, we turn to this question of when something is unethical in modern financial markets. As discussed in the preceding chapter, the evolution of finance has brought about the fracturing of component cash flows, which in turn allows for the creation of myriad types of securities, contracts, and investment opportunities. In this environment, complexity reigns, and the "big picture" may be indiscernible to all but the most sophisticated. An added complication is that exactly who is on the "other side" of contracts is opaque, obscured by the layers of positions involved. This impersonality of markets, in turn, makes it easy to ignore or not even see the harm done to other parties. It should not be surprising that perceiving where the ethical boundaries lie is similarly problematic.

There has always been a variety of approaches for discerning when something "crosses the line," ranging from religious beliefs to legal strictures to philosophical foundations to ethical culture arguments. Doing justice to the moral frameworks suggested by any of these approaches is clearly beyond the scope of this book. Instead, I attempt the more modest task of considering how each approach views the simple question of when something is unacceptable behavior. Building from this, we can then turn to the larger question of how to discern the ethical dimensions of arbitrage in modern financial markets.

"Fear of God" and Ethical Behavior

> Outdo one another in showing honor.
>
> —ROMANS 12:10

When asked about the secret to his success, George Gilbert Williams, who became president of the Chemical Bank in 1878, answered succinctly: the "fear of God."[1] The notion that a failure to act ethically would elicit divine retribution is surely a motivator for ethical behavior. And for those with religious beliefs, the issues of ethics and religion are so intertwined as to be inseparable. Indeed, Simon Blackburn notes, "For many people, ethics is not only tied up with religion, but is completely settled by it. Such people do not need to think too much about ethics, because there is an authoritative code of instructions, a handbook of how to live."[2]

In this regard, it is interesting to contemplate how universal are the dictums regarding ethical behavior arising from disparate religious beliefs. Surely Mr. Gilbert would have subscribed to the Golden Rule, so central to Christian beliefs: "Do unto others as you would have them do unto you" (Matthew 7:12). But a similar teaching runs through a wide range of world religions.[3] Confucianism, for example, enjoins its followers, "Do not unto others what you do not want them to do to you" (Analects 15:13). Sikhism instructs, "Treat others as thou wouldst be treated thyself" (Adi Granth). Jainism says, "A man should wander about treating all creatures as he himself would be treated" (Sutrakritanga 1:11:33). Taoism teaches, "Regard your neighbor's gain as your own gain and your neighbor's loss as your own loss." The Quran directs the followers of Islam. "Deal not unjustly and you shall not be dealt with unjustly" (Quran 2:279). Judaism instructs, "That which is despicable to you, do not do to your fellow, this is the whole of the Torah, and the rest is commentary. Go and learn it" (Hillel). There seems to be a common theme here!

That religious belief dictates ethical behavior certainly is true for many people, although its influences may have been more engrained in earlier, less secular times. Still, the notion that there is a "higher law" that governs behavior can be found in many settings. John Locke, for example, argued that every man has "inalienable rights" that cannot be taken away, because they come from a higher law (i.e., God). This higher law was the basis for his views on the proper roles (and behavior) of man and government in society.[4] Similar presuppositions are echoed in the U.S. Constitution and its "we hold these truths to be self-evident." Even Adam Smith, famous for his invisible hand of the market, noted in *The Theory of Moral Sentiments* that "the role of the care of the universal happiness of all rational and sensible beings is the business of God and not of man." So here, too, there is a higher authority beyond what simply goes on in the market.

Getting from the "fear of God" to what is actually required for ethical behavior, however, is not always clear-cut. Islamic finance provides some interesting guidance with respect to this in its directives regarding the types of contracts prohibited in Islamic commercial and financial transactions. In particular, Islamic finance prohibits *gharar*, or uncertainty. As Harris Irfan, one of the leading experts on Islamic finance, explains, "uncertainty in sales and other transactions is considered to void or invalidate a contract, and may indicate that the party practicing it is deceiving or defrauding his counterparty, and indeed cheating and fraud are generally considered to be special cases of *gharar*. It arises when there is a lack of knowledge of the subject matter. . . ."[5] He goes on to note that Islamic scholars, such as Mahmoud El-Gamal, argue that *gharar* can be a result of "one-sided or two-sided and intentional or unintentional incompleteness of information."[6] As we will discuss in later chapters, the complexity of modern finance can introduce exactly such asymmetries in information between parties. At least for adherents of Islam, the exploiting of such asymmetries is unethical.

Modern financial markets are also characterized by impersonality, as buyers and sellers are often many stages removed in the process of exchange. With only an amorphous entity somewhere on the other side, admonitions for participants to "do unto others" may seem at best nebulous, and at worst inapplicable. What is not so amorphous for those with religious convictions, however, is the basic requirement to consider the moral impact of economic decisions. Pope Benedict XVI, in the encyclical *Caritas in Veritate* (2009), argued that "to discern the common good and to strive for it is a requirement of justice and charity. . . . This is the institutional path—we might call it the political path—of charity, no less excellent and effective than the kind of charity which encounters the neighbor directly. . . ."[7]

This obligation to "discern the common good" borrows from earlier writers who focused on the obligation to build "the city of God" through righteous behavior. It seems a particularly appropriate admonition in modern market settings, for it suggests that actions that degrade the integrity of the overall market, that impose harm on other people, even though they may be unidentified, are unethical. It also suggests that a good financier is not just someone who is setting up "deals," but rather is one who contributes to the effective functioning of the market in carrying out its role in society. Indeed, Pope Benedict XVI went on to maintain, "Financiers must rediscover the genuinely ethical foundations of their activity, so as not to abuse the sophisticated instruments which can serve to betray the interests of savers." Or, put another way, "It is not the instrument that must be called to account, but the individual, their moral conscience and personal responsibility."[8]

While such a focus might be expected from the pope, an almost identical sentiment has been expressed by Mark Carney, the head of the Bank of England. He laments, "a malaise in the corners of finance that must be remedied."[9] He argues that "financiers, like all of us, need to avoid compartmentalisation—the division of our lives into different realms, each with its own set of rules. Home is distinct from work, ethics from law, the individual from the system." Instead, those in finance have an obligation to rebuild the "social capital" of the free-market system.

This focus on the ethical foundations of financial activity, on individuals' responsibility to take account of the moral impact of their actions, suggests that what was true for Mr. Gilbert in a simpler time remains true today. Ethical behavior should be the guiding principle of financial practice because failure to do so falls short of what is morally required.

A Legal View of Ethical Behavior

A more worldly view is that ethical behavior in markets is determined by a legal standard, not a moral one. From this perspective, participants in markets are free to behave as they wish, enjoined only by explicit legal prohibitions against fraud and other proscribed behaviors. In some markets settings, such prohibitions are lacking, and contracting between agents is governed by the maxim "caveat emptor" (buyer beware). In other settings, a norm of expected behavior, often referred to as the morals of the market, prevails, precluding outright criminality, but usually little else.

This "morals of the marketplace" concept gained prominence when used by Justice Benjamin Cardozo in his famous decision in *Meinhard v. Salmon*.[10] This case involved a dispute over the obligations partners in a business owe to one another when a business opportunity arises in the course of the partnership. Justice Cardozo argued that, unlike regular participants in the market, "a trustee is held to something stricter than the morals of the marketplace. Not honesty alone, but the punctilio of an honor the most sensitive, is then the standard of behavior." Thus, while honesty is expected of all, some participants (in this case, the partners) face a higher ethical standard in connection with their duties as fiduciaries.

But exactly what is this higher ethical standard? An equally famous statement by Justice Felix Frankfurter points out the challenges here: "To say that a man is a fiduciary only begins the analysis: it gives direction for further inquiry. To whom is he a fiduciary? What obligations does he owe as a fiduciary? And what are the consequences of his deviation from duty?"[11] So detailing exactly what this behavior should be is problematic, in part because it requires understanding more about specific circumstances that may not easily be articulated in advance. In this sense, fiduciary duties are sometimes viewed as "filling in the holes" in contracts by instead requiring particular duties for fiduciaries. These duties include a duty of care and a duty of loyalty, and essentially impose a legal obligation on one party to act in the best interests of another. If you are not a fiduciary, however, you face no such obligation—anything (short of dishonesty) goes.

The view that ethical behavior includes everything except the strictly illegal is a defensible, but surely limited, standard. One difficulty with such a view is that it misses the point, learned by Bankers Trust and countless others, that simply being legal does not make behavior trustworthy. Confucious, writing in the fifth century BCE, instructed besieged rulers that if necessary first give up weapons, and then food, but hang on to trust at all costs because "without trust we cannot stand."[12] Given that trust becomes increasingly important as complexity increases, such a conclusion seems particularly relevant for today's complex financial markets. A variety of research shows convincingly that when trust is absent, so is participation in financial markets.[13] Why enter into a contract if you do not trust your counterparty? A viable ethical standard must surely be one that requires more than simply not being a felon!

A second problem with a strict legal standard is that almost by definition the law will lag behind the market. This is because markets innovate in ways that can make prior practices obsolete, rendering the laws and rules designed to regulate market practices and behaviors outdated and ineffective. New laws are then enacted, but in the time it takes to do so the market has moved on again, leaving the regulators (and the legal structure) always a step behind. The problem with a legal standard is not with the law per se, but rather with the laws that should, but do not yet, exist.

This regulatory rat race is surely more of a problem in the arbitrage-based world of modern finance. As the *Economist* noted, "regulators cannot hold the line forever. Ultimately, they are likely to lose ground to financiers who will use arbitrage to work their way around the best-laid defenses."[14] Indeed, as we will discuss in chapter 7, a major use of arbitrage is to circumvent impediments in markets, some of which arise from regulation. The point here is not that arbitrage is unethical (recall that buying low and selling high is not a moral statement). Rather, it is that an ethical standard linked solely to a legal standard seems destined to be deficient.

An interesting feature of regulation in modern security markets is disclosure requirements. Such disclosure rules were intended to level the playing field between buyers and sellers of securities, thereby reducing the ability of sellers to take advantage of uninformed buyers. Disclosure requirements also shift the onus for determining what must be disclosed from the regulators to the sellers of securities, who must disclose all "material information." The SEC commissioner Dan Gallagher in a recent speech highlighted how such disclosure rules play a role in ensuring ethical behavior. In particular, he cited President Franklin Roosevelt's message to Congress that disclosure "adds to the ancient rule of caveat emptor, the further doctrine, 'let the seller also beware.' It puts the burden of telling the whole truth on the seller. It should give impetus to honest dealing in securities and thereby bring back public confidence."[15]

This notion that acceptable behavior is not strictly about "what you have done but what you have failed to do" gives the legal basis for ethical behavior greater scope. But as Commissioner Gallagher points out, the positive intent of disclosure regulation can be thwarted by its implementation. In particular, when companies provide hundreds of pages of disclosures, detailing every possible risk that could or might occur, it is confusion rather than clarity that prevails. That is unlikely to lead to the "honest dealing" and "public confidence" in markets noted above. The flip side of this problem for companies is to sort out what is "material" to disclose. Much like the minutiae on Facebook (does anyone really care what you had for lunch?), some corporate information is not worth sharing, while other things are. And when you do share, you may find yourself in the odd position that Goldman Sachs encountered when it was sued by some investors who claimed that its disclosed code of ethics was "fraudulent." The lack of clarity here suggests yet another limitation to a purely legal basis for ethical behavior.

Implementation issues also arise with respect to the enforcement of laws. While the threat of eternal damnation may sufficiently motivate ethical behavior in a religious context, the prospect of possible prosecution is much less daunting. Indeed, despite Attorney General Eric Holder's stern video warning that no banker is "too big to jail," the fact that only one banker has actually gone to jail in the aftermath of the recent financial crisis provides little deterrence to illegal behavior.[16] In such a world, the legal standard does not establish the lines of acceptable behavior; instead, it simply sets in motion an explicit calculation of the costs and benefits of illegality. A joke circulating at the time of the Michael Milken trial captured this problem: "Two years in jail, $560 million in profits: I'd take that trade." Perhaps it is not surprising that financial crime has flourished in this environment, driven by a calculus that finds the probability of actual punishment too low to influence behavior.

Philosophical Foundations of Ethical Behavior

In the search for a framework to define ethical behavior, it is natural to turn to the philosophers for whom the nature of ethics has been a central question. From Aristotle to Kant to more current truth seekers (Scott Adams and Dilbert come to mind), setting out what constitutes ethical behavior has been a long-standing quest. While any serious review of philosophical theories of ethics is far beyond our purview here, it is useful to think about the general approaches to the issue of how to determine the right thing to do. Michael Sandel, in his superb book *Justice: What's the Right Thing to Do?*, argues that this topic has typically been addressed within three general frameworks: virtue, welfare, and freedom.[17] Indeed, he points out that "ancient theories of justice start with virtue, while more modern theories start with freedom," though he is quick to add that most ethical frameworks are rarely one-dimensional.

Aristotelian views on the importance of virtue ("All virtue is summed up in dealing justly") share important links to our earlier section on religious frameworks. In our modern context, Aristotle's specific focus on the roles of technique and prudence is particularly intriguing. In his masterwork *Ethics*, Aristotle argues that technique concerns itself with making, while prudence concerns itself with human actions in general.[18] As such, technique can be viewed as abstracting from ethical issues because its only concern is with the "making" of something—for example, structuring a contract. As Andrew Yuengert explains, however, "technique is never applied in the abstract. It is carried out as part of a project of action in pursuit of someone's ends."[19] These ends are the focus of prudence—it orders our actions to maximize happiness and so brings into focus the "morally relevant qualities of the person who acts." For Aristotle, focusing only on technique misses the moral component—the ethical component—which gives prudence governance over technique. Every technical action thus has a moral component, and this moral component requires the pursuit of virtue. For Aristotle, arbitrage is not just a technique but rather an action with an intrinsic moral component.

The more "modern" approaches—I will focus here on consequential approaches and categorical approaches—view morality through a different lens. The consequential approach determines the morality of an action as depending solely on the consequences it brings. In its strictest form, it dictates that the right thing to do is whatever will maximize the collective happiness of society as a whole.[20] This approach, first proposed by Jeremy Bentham and more generally identified as utilitarianism, holds that "the highest principle of morality is to maximize happiness" and that this involves maximizing utility. Such utility maximization should apply both to individual actions and to collective actions in that the government should pass laws that serve to maximize the happiness of the community. For utilitarians, what matters is the greatest good for the greatest numbers.

Some of Bentham's views would today surely seem extreme. For example, he argued for "pauper management" in which paupers would be rounded up and sent to workhouses, thereby sparing everyone else the disagreeable task having to encounter them in the streets. The inconvenience felt by the paupers was viewed as a reasonable price to pay for the positive overall net effect on society as a whole. Still, though the workhouses are now long gone, there are rather eerie similarities between this philosophy and the "squeegee man" campaigns of New York City in the last decade.

For an individual, the notion of choosing actions that lead to the greatest level of his or her own happiness seems a reasonable course of action (and it is what we generally teach in economics courses). Self-interest, however, is not enough to meet the moral requirements of utilitarianism. Actions must be evaluated with respect to their effects on the "overall happiness" of society. Yet, for society as a whole, viewing the world from a utilitarian perspective can lead to perverse outcomes because this philosophy attaches no weight to the rights of an individual. Consider, for example, whether it would be ethical to cheat a little girl selling lemonade from a front yard stand? If the child does not really know that she has been cheated, then she is not really worse-off. And if you can benefit by having both the lemonade and the money, then you are clearly better-off. A "win, win" so to speak! Or, more to the topic at hand, would a broker's taking advantage of an unsophisticated client (who may not even realize he has been cheated) be acceptable behavior provided that the broker's actions did not bring down the entire market (and thereby make everyone worse-off)? From a pure utilitarian perspective, it would seem so. And yet, simply looking at the "greatest good" seems to miss something important.

These difficulties are related to a second objection to utilitarianism: it is not clear how to aggregate various utilities across people. As Michael Sandel explains, "Utilitarianism claims to offer a science of morality, based on measuring, aggregating, and calculating happiness. It weighs preferences without judging them. Everyone's preferences count equally. . . . But is it possible to translate all moral goods into a single currency of value without losing something in the translation?"[21]

To illustrate this problem, Sandel poses the question of the morality of killing people for organs. If one person could provide organs to save five lives, would not society be better-off by sacrificing the one to save the many? Although on a strictly utilitarian basis perhaps the answer is yes, few people would feel comfortable with a world in which you could be "harvested" for the greater good. Many economists would argue that the problem here is that utilities are simply not measurable across people.[22] While we would all agree that an action which makes one person better-off without harming anyone else is acceptable,[23] this does not mean that an action that makes many people better-off at the cost of harming someone else makes society better-off. How do we know that the harm created to that one person doesn't far outweigh the benefits enjoyed by the others?

Alternatively, one could argue, as Sandel does, that the metric for calculating the greater good is deficient because it did not recognize all of the consequences of an action. If people stop going to doctors, for example, because they are afraid of becoming a "donor," then all of society is worse-off, and so this is not a moral outcome. This broader perspective of including all of an action's consequences in this moral calculation provides a way to rehabilitate at least part of this ethical framework. Now, cheating someone in the market may not be ethical if over time it leads to a loss of confidence and therefore decreased participation in the markets. Being able to foresee all of an action's consequences, however, seems a formidable task, particularly if those consequences play out over time. Moreover, the problem in economics of "unintended consequences" is well known, since actions may cause perverse effects to arise far from the market setting of the original action. Using consequences to gauge the morality of an action seems a challenging metric to employ.

By contrast, the categorical approach disagrees with the contention that only consequences matter and argues that certain duties and obligations prevail—that some things are simply wrong. The leading proponent of this school of thought, Immanuel Kant, would say that a categorical duty is one that applies regardless of circumstance. Since it always applies, some things are unconditionally wrong. For Kant "the moral worth of an action consists not in the consequences that flow from it, but in the intention from which the act is done. What matters is the motive, and the motive must be of a certain kind. What matters is doing the right thing because it is right, not for some ulterior motive."[24]

But what types of motives are the "right" kind, and, equally important, how does one know when something is categorically wrong? For Kant, the answer lies in the concept of human dignity. Kant argues that respecting human dignity requires treating each person as an end in himself or herself.[25] Thus, while one might be tempted to cheat someone if the benefits outweigh the costs (the ends justify the means, so to speak), for Kant such a calculation is irrelevant. It is individuals who matter as ends in themselves, so it is not okay to justify actions in the name of the general welfare. When you cheat, you place your needs and desires above everyone else, and that is not acceptable, regardless of how well it turns out for everyone else.

For Kant "it is not enough that it [an action] should conform to the moral law—it must also be done for the sake of the moral law." Indeed, Sandel argues that "the motive that confers moral worth on an action is the motive of duty, by which Kant means doing the right things for the right reason."[26] Other motives, no matter how well they accord with the desired outcome, lack "moral worth." For Kant, a broker who treats a customer fairly because not doing so undermines future business from that customer and others is not acting morally, because his motive is self-interest rather than duty. Similarly, Sandel gives the example of an ad in the *New York Times* run by the Better Business Bureau of New York stating, "Honesty is the best policy. It's also the most profitable."[27] Kant would surely not be impressed.

Kant's focus on the human being as an end in itself is the basis for his categorical imperative—"Act in such a way that you always treat humanity, whether in your own person or in the person of any other, never simply as a means, but always at the same time as an end." Earlier we discussed the Aristotelian mandate to pursue virtue by treating all justly and the "fear of God" arguments that dictated, "Treat thy neighbor as thyself." While seemingly similar to Kant's exhortation, the motives behind these approaches are not the same, even though the outcomes may be very similar. For Kant, however, that motive makes all the difference.

There are, of course, more modern philosophical discourses on moral behavior, such as John Rawls's *A Theory of Justice* or Robert Nozick's *Anarchy, State, and Utopia*.[28] As my goal here is not a philosophy review, I think discussion of these views takes me too far afield from my purpose of discerning when something is acceptable behavior. What may be more fruitful to consider are modern approaches of a less formal, or "folk," nature, and these fall under the general rubric of ethical culture.

Ethical Culture and Ethical Behavior

For some people, neither the complexity of philosophy nor the theology underlying religious beliefs resonate with their views regarding the nature of ethical behavior in society. Instead, a more secular, informal approach consistent with the notion that ethical behavior is a natural outgrowth of leading a meaningful life is more amenable. The Ethical Culture movement is one manifestation of such an approach, and like the other perspectives we have considered, it provides a prescription for determining when something crosses the lines of acceptable behavior.

The Ethical Culture movement is "premised on the idea that honoring and living in accordance with ethical principles is central to what it takes to live meaningful and fulfilling lives, and to creating a world that is good for all."[29] Although some trace this movement back to Victorian times and the establishment of groups like the Fabian Society, its modern embodiment is generally ascribed to Felix Adler and his founding of the New York Society for Ethical Culture in the late nineteenth century. A decentralized movement followed as ethical societies proliferated across the United States, many of which remain in existence. Today, less formal entities, such as the Foundation for a Better Life (perhaps best known for its "Pass it on" commercials and billboards), seem to me to share much of this ethical perspective.

Fundamental to an ethical culture perspective is Adler's view that society is made up of unique moral agents (aka people) who each have "inestimable influence" on each other. This interrelatedness is at the heart of ethics. Ethical culture societies generally subscribe to the view captured in the Ethical Culture 2003 identity statement that "if we relate to others in a way that brings out their best, we will at the same time elicit the best in ourselves." Moreover, "when we act to elicit the best in others, we encourage the growing edge of their ethical development, their perhaps as-yet untapped but inexhaustible worth."[30]

Ethics is central to this perspective, but what exactly is ethical is less well defined. That is because "what is right or wrong, good or bad, is so because it fosters the development of what is best in life." What may be "best," however, evolves over time, reflecting that "ethics begins with judgment and choice . . . and the values and principles that guide our choices rest on a natural interpretation of experience."[31] Because individuals will have different experiences, the final arbiter of what is ethical is the individual.[32] Such a perspective may have informed a witticism allegedly uttered by Bertrand Russell, "Do not do unto others what you would have them do unto you, because their tastes may be different!"[33]

Differences notwithstanding, there are some common beliefs that are held to be foundational. One of these is that ethics is not relative: some actions are wrong and are recognized as such by all. A second precept is to treat all individuals as ends and not as means. Both of these we have already encountered in Kant's categorical approach. A third is the specific commitment to treat one another fairly.[34] These shared beliefs, combined with the role played by individual conscience, mean that there is a right or wrong for every individual, although recognizing it may be problematic. We consider this complication in chapter 10 when we discuss the emergent field of behavioral ethics.

This linking of fairness and ethics seems almost universal, playing a central role for Aristotle as well as for every three-year-old who ever uttered the phrase "that's not fair." In financial markets, the notion of fairness is fundamental to a wide variety of regulatory constructs, such as insider-trading prohibitions, fair access to market data requirements, and even recent attempts to curtail high-frequency trading. As we will discuss in the coming chapters, fairness as an ethical concept often determines for many people whether something crosses the lines of acceptable behavior.

Thus, whether you start from a religious, legal, philosophical, or even cultural foundation, the practical implications for ethical behavior of each actually arrive at many of the same end points. The notions of treating others fairly, of there being some common good that we should endeavor to attain, or of there being some things that are wrong (either because of a human law or of a higher law arising from a higher power or not) all speak to a need to recognize the impact of our actions beyond ourselves—in other words, to behave ethically.

CHAPTER 5

ETHICS IN ACTION

These are my principles. If you don't like them, I have others.

—GROUCHO MARX[1]

WHERE DO YOU draw the line between acceptable and unacceptable activities? As we have seen, the various perspectives developed in the last chapter all give guidance as to where the "lines" defining acceptable behavior lie in modern markets. These lines are not always the same, but there is basic agreement that some activities cross into the unacceptable realm. Agreeing that such lines exist in principle, however, and actually behaving accordingly in practice are two different things. A particular complication is that individuals rarely operate in a vacuum but are part of larger entities such as corporations. A related challenge is that arbitrage activity often takes place in markets. Do the ethical "rules" applying at the individual level have similar relevance at the corporate or market level?

Ethical Boundaries in the Workplace

If your job is to maximize shareholder value, why do you care about the ethical considerations of a deal? Indeed, can you care? One of the most cited articles in the *Harvard Business Review*, Albert Carr's "Is Business Bluffing Ethical?," posed this question, and its answer set the stage for countless debates in business school ethics classes ever since.[2] Carr argued that the successful businessman must be guided by a "different set of ethical standards," that "the ethics of business are game ethics, different from the ethics of religion." Comparing business to a poker game, he held that "the major tests of every move in business are legality and profit." If something is not strictly illegal, and it can be profitable, then it is the obligation of the businessman to pursue it.

That legality alone determines what is ethical in business is not a new idea. Indeed, some interpreted a famous statement in Milton Friedman's *Capitalism and Freedom* as saying exactly that: "there is one and only one social responsibility of business—to use its resources and engage in activities designed to increase its profits so long as it stays within the rules of the game, which is to say, engages in open and free competition, without deception or fraud."[3] Yet Friedman was not so dogmatic about the singular role of legality, clarifying in his article "The Social Responsibility of Business Is to Increase Profits" that the responsibility of the corporate executive "will be to make as much money as possible while conforming to the basic rules of society, both those embodied in law and *those embodied in ethical custom*."[4]

It is safe to say that Carr missed this latter point as he pushed this concept of legality-only to extremes. He noted, for example, that "the golden rule, for all its virtues as an ideal for society, is simply not feasible as a guide for business. A good part of the time the businessman is trying to do to others as he hopes others will not do unto him." Moreover, he argued, "If the ethics aren't embodied in the laws by the men who made them, you can't expect businessmen to fill the gap." Carr then listed a variety of practices that would be perfectly acceptable under this dictum, such as corporate espionage, producing and selling defective automobiles, selling tainted produce, selling master keys to criminals, and helping foreign customers evade taxes in their home countries.

Reading the Carr article today is eye-opening. Certainly, his list of acceptable practices seems dated, and it highlights how much things change over time.[5] In one sense, this is consistent with his theory—laws reflect moral standards, and over time the laws change to reflect what is acceptable to society. The items on his acceptable list would now all be on the wrong side of this divide. But that also highlights why a strategy of being exactly on the line of legality is a poor business practice; when lines shift, you go from being a weasel to being a felon, even when you have done nothing differently. The recent plethora of fines and settlements at financial firms testifies to how quickly industry practices (such as setting LIBOR) can convert into regulatory transgressions. The price of over $127 billion (and counting) in fines and settlements for large U.S. banks since 2008 demonstrates how expensive this transition can be.

Carr's arguments have been criticized from a variety of perspectives. Some critics contend that linking business practice only to law misses the point that law is rooted in ordinary morality and draws its moral authority from that consistency. Philosophers and theologians alike have held that law (or human law) and morality (natural law) are inextricably linked. Aquinas, for example, believed that the purpose of human law is the common good, and the promotion of virtue, fundamental to Aristotle's views, was a necessary part of this.[6] Carr's argument that only the law matters misses this nexus of law and morality—if morality determines the law and law determines business practices, why doesn't morality also apply to business practices? And if only the law determines business practices, does this mean that we need new laws to define the boundaries around every aspect of business behavior? Is this even possible?

Others raise the issue of the fiction of the corporate entity. Dana Radcliffe provides a thoughtful perspective on this issue in his article "Should Companies Obey the Law If Breaking It Is More Profitable?"[7] He starts by noting Robert Reich's argument "that companies are 'neither moral nor immoral,' being 'logical fictions, nothing more than bundles of contractual agreements.' Because they are not 'moral entities,' as human beings are, they are not proper objects of moral demands or criticisms."[8] Radcliffe counters, however, that "a corporation is not simply a 'bundle of contracts' but is an organization consisting of assorted individuals occupying contract-governed roles." Thus, while the corporation may be a legal fiction, the individuals who act for it are not—and they are governed by moral obligations.

Yet others have disagreed with the basic premise that it is good business to be guided only by legality and profits. Jonathan Macey, in his book *The Death of Corporate Reputation*, argues that "corporate finance and capital markets traditionally relied heavily on the ability of companies and other firms to develop what is known as reputational capital."[9] Reputations for fair dealing, trustworthiness, and the like were viewed as a corporate asset, an investment vital to the ability of the firm to flourish in the long run. This point was driven home by Warren Buffett's much-cited testimony to a House Committee upon his taking over management at Salomon Brothers: "Lose money for the firm and I will be understanding; lose a shred of reputation for the firm and I will be ruthless."[10]

Whether reputation still plays such a pivotal role is debatable. Macey argues that it does not, driven out by factors such as the shift in financial firms away from ongoing relationship-based business to more episodic transaction-based activities. Why build a reputation for fair dealing in the long term if your relationship with clients is "one and done"? Others have argued that reputation likely plays a role where customers feel they have a real choice, where dishonesty is knowable, and where behavior among competitors is clearly distinguishable. It is debatable whether the current oligopolistic structure of Wall Street banks meets these conditions. Perhaps this gap between theory and reality is at the heart of Alan Greenspan's statement: "Those of us who have looked to the self-interest of lending institutions to protect shareholder's equity, myself included, are in a state of shocked disbelief."[11]

Macey also contends that the demise of reputation is due, in part, to the changing nature of regulation. Following deregulation in the 1980s, banks were free to pay market interest rates, compete in new areas, and devise new financial products. But regulations for banks in other areas such as anti-money-laundering rules, complex capital requirements, and consumer lending protections expanded dramatically, with rules applying to seemingly every activity (and for the largest banks, embedded regulators to make sure you are following them). Despite this increased focus, Macey argues, the financial crisis has demonstrated anew that "regulation is no substitute for reputation in ensuring contractual performance and respect for property rights."

The current regulatory focus on "culture" issues in banking suggests that regulators share a similar concern with respect to the efficacy of regulation alone to ensure ethical behavior.[12] Their demand that banking institutions develop ethical cultures suggests that corporations are not immune to ethical considerations. But whether culture is any more robust than reputation for dealing with greed and agency issues within the firm that give rise to unethical behavior is unclear. Certainly, it is no easier to measure (how much ethical culture do we have? Is it increasing or is it decreasing?), nor is it clear how to sort out whether we have the "right" culture or the "wrong" one. We return to these culture issues in chapter 10. For now, however, it seems evident that the maximizing of shareholder value does not provide a free pass to unethical behavior for either the company or the people who work there.

Ethical Boundaries in the Market

If the market is for consenting adults. why should you ever care about the person on the other side of a trade? Certainly, anyone who participates in the market accepts that some trades (and traders) will win and some will lose. Arbitrage is also motivated by expectation of gain—why take positions if there is not some expected recompense? As I have noted before, buying low and selling high does not involve a moral judgment, and being able to recognize profitable trading opportunities is a plus, not a minus. But this does not mean that "anything goes" in a market. Selling "phony" or nonexistent securities, for example, is both illegal and unethical. Misrepresenting important features of the item being traded (i.e., fraud), or trading so as to manipulate the market are similarly unacceptable practices. Losing to a skilled trader is not evidence of unethical behavior, but being cheated by one is.

Often one party in a trade has better information, or more

expertise, than its counterparty. This is the natural state for a market. If everyone agreed, the motivations for trade would be severely limited. In some cases, though, this disparity is too great to be acceptable. Duping small, naïve investors into buying unsuitable financial products, for example, has long been viewed as unethical, and such trading is generally prohibited. But for others, how unequal does the disparity have to be to cross this line? Gibson Greetings successfully argued that Bankers Trust took advantage of an "unknowing customer," pushing the line farther out to include at least some corporate counterparties. As we will see in chapter 7, the SEC argued that Goldman Sachs essentially did the same thing in a different transaction, even though the counterparties in question were generally other, presumably sophisticated financial institutions. The legal line over what constitutes acceptable behavior between unequal counterparties is clearly shifting.

This suggests that while every player in poker is considered fair game, the same cannot always be said of every trader in a financial transaction. Economists have long recognized that if information becomes too asymmetric, and people capitalize on it too much, then markets can "break" in the sense that no one is willing to buy anything that someone else is willing to sell.[13] This "markets for lemons" problem underscores the practical limits of being too opportunistic in markets: at some point, no one will trade with you.

But should ethics play no role in markets before we reach that breaking point? Many in economics would agree with this prescription, arguing that markets work best when left to their own devices. For example, Kenneth Arrow, a Nobel laureate in the field, wrote, "Like many economists, I do not want to rely too heavily on substituting ethics for self-interest. I think it best on the whole that the requirement of ethical behavior be confined to those circumstances where the price system breaks down."[14] This view of ethics as a last resort, as an overlay needed only when the system is broken, draws on a tradition in economics of viewing the outcome arising from the maximizing behavior of traders as optimal. That is, given the rules of the market, each trader is free to take his or her best action—and that leads to the best overall outcome.

But is this always true? Markets often feature strategic behavior, and in a strategic setting there is no reason to expect that the equilibrium outcome will yield a socially optimal allocation. Indeed, even the notion of equilibrium is different in a strategic setting as each person has to think about the strategies that will be used by all the other players. This insight led John Nash to formulate the Nash equilibrium concept, in which each player selects a strategy that is optimal, given the strategies of the other players.[15] But no force exists to guarantee that the players select strategies that maximize joint payoffs. This nonoptimality occurs, for example, in a prisoner's dilemma game in which although each player has a dominant strategy, the pair of dominant strategies can yield a minimum of the sum of payoffs rather than a maximum.

More generally, strategic interactions can yield multiple equilibria. Some of these equilibria are "better" in that they make someone better-off without making anyone else worse-off (what economists call Pareto optimal). But other equilibria can exist—equilibria in which the bad outcome rather than the good outcome prevails. This problem can be illustrated with a simple example of a two-person game in which the players' payoffs will differ depending upon the strategy they select. Each player may be deciding whether to participate in a bank run and withdraw money, or wait and leave the money in the bank.[16]

Figure 6 shows a simple payoff matrix in which player 1

chooses a row (run or don't run) and player 2 chooses a column (run or don't run). If neither player runs, then they each get a payoff of 100, reflecting that the bank can leave assets to mature and so suffer no loss. If either player chooses to run, then his payoff is 50 if the other player does not run, and the one who does not run gets zero. If both players run, then they each get a payoff of 20. These lower numbers reflect the problem that the bank will have to sell assets to get money to pay depositors and the more they have to liquidate, the bigger are the losses.

In games like this, the Nash equilibrium is found by evaluating each player's choice as the best response to the other player's choice. Thus, it is easy to see that if player 1 believes that player 2 will not run, then his best response is also to not run (he gets 100 if he does not run and 50 if he does). However, if player 1 believes that player 2 will run, then his best response is also to run, since he gets 20 if he runs and 0 if he does not run. Because player 2's payoffs are symmetric, he follows similar reasoning. So there are actually two (pure strategy) Nash equilibria in this game—run if you think the other guy runs and don't run if you think he won't run.[17]

Figure 6

Payoffs in a Two-Person Game

1 \ 2	Run	Not-Run
Run	20, 20	50, 0
Not-Run	0, 50	100, 100

Both players have to choose whether to run or not run. Player 1 chooses a row, and player 2 chooses a column. In each cell of the matrix, the first number is player 1's payoff, and the second number is player 2's payoff.

The bank run game illustrates an important point: coordination on the socially best equilibrium would make both players better-off, but there is nothing in the equilibrium concept that guarantees this outcome. Consequently, a bank run can emerge in equilibrium and, in a different setting, so could an equilibrium in which both traders cheat in submitting LIBOR bids rather than report honestly. Of course, not cheating can also be an equilibrium, and forces such as social or ethical norms may be valuable in helping players coordinate on socially desirable outcomes.

Even in nonstrategic settings, however, the conventional wisdom in economics that a competitive equilibrium is Pareto optimal may not hold. This is because the assumptions (this is economics after all!) needed for this to occur are extensive and unlikely to hold in many markets. The optimal result requires perfectly competitive markets in which no person's actions directly affect prices. The high-frequency markets discussed in chapter 8, for example, do not fit this description, nor would the myriad markets in which dealer market power can affect trading prices. Indeed, it is not even clear how markets as we know them at all fit here, because prices in the competitive equilibrium just appear and equate supply and demand. Actual prices often depend upon the rules and practices in the markets or what is called the market microstructure. Changing those rules can change prices, and some microstructures can result in very poor market outcomes (an issue we also discuss in chapter 7, in the context of the California electricity markets). The prescription that if you don't like the outcome just change the rules misses the point that the new outcome may not be anywhere near optimality either.

Yet another assumption within the standard economics approach is that preferences are taken as given and that social welfare is evaluated according to whatever preferences people happen to have. There is no discussion of better or worse preferences, or of ones that we might regard as simply mistaken, or of how social norms or ethics can change these preferences and the outcomes that would otherwise prevail. These issues all reflect the same problem—the market may find an equilibrium, but relying on it to be an "optimal" one requires a leap of faith that may not be justified in many market settings. Indeed, there is even a large literature debating whether it is possible, or desirable, to put an equilibrium price on everything—kidneys, blood donations, and children are oft-debated examples. The point here is that eschewing a role for ethics in markets because the price system will do just fine on its own in sorting things out correctly is just too simplistic.

Economics has also long recognized that markets can fail in the presence of externalities. An externality arises when the social costs (or benefits) of an action do not equal the private costs (or benefits). Thus, a factory will underinvest in pollution control activities if it does not take account of (or is not required to compensate for) the harm done to the surrounding community by the pollution spewing from its smokestacks. Pursuing trading strategies that lead to individual gain but can destabilize an entire market is not really any different; such behavior can "break" markets because individuals do not appropriately balance the total costs and benefits of their actions.

Michael Lewis, in his book *Liar's Poker*, tells the anecdote of how Lewis Ranieri ran trading at Salomon Brothers. "At other places, management says, 'Well, gee, fellas, do we really want to bet the ranch on this deal? . . . His [Ranieri's] attitude was: 'Sure, what the fuck, it's only a ranch.'"[18] One may perhaps not care too much about ranches, but is the same true when we talk about the market? Is it ethical to enter into trades that can destabilize or take down the entire market? Certainly from the religious, Aristotelian, consequential, or categorical perspectives, the answer is no, and, given the externality imposed, even economics would agree with that conclusion.

Mark Carney, the head of the Bank of England, makes another case for why the answer is no.[19] He argues that "for markets to sustain their legitimacy, they need to be not only effective but also *fair*. Nowhere is that need more acute than in financial markets; finance has to be *trusted*." This focus on fairness recalls the themes of ethical culture discussed in the preceding chapter (and, for that matter, the sage advice of Confucius in 500 BCE). Indeed, in order for this trust in finance to occur, Carney calls for an "inclusive capitalism" in which "individuals and their firms must have a sense of their responsibilities for the broader system. . . . By building a sense of responsibility for the system, individuals will act in ways that reinforce the bonds of social capital and inclusive capitalism." For Carney, "a sense of self must be accompanied by a sense of the systemic."[20]

An interesting question is whether such responsibility can simply be imposed by regulation. In September 2014, the major U.S. futures exchanges, at the urging of their regulator, the CFTC (Commodity Futures Trading Commission), enacted rules explicitly prohibiting market destabilizing behavior in futures markets.[21] Rule 575 details a list of specified behaviors, many of which we will discuss in chapter 8, that are now prohibited. The problem remains, however, that it is not always a straightforward task to detect such behavior in today's high-frequency markets, and that leads to the enforcement difficulties noted earlier. More to the point, Carney argues that "social capital is not contractual; integrity can neither be bought nor regulated." This suggests that, regulations notwithstanding, ethical obligations attach to market outcomes. Hence, while betting the ranch may or may not be ethical, betting the market is not.

Where Do You Draw the Line?

Whether you build on religious, legal, philosophical, or cultural foundations, there are clearly boundaries that define ethical behavior. While these approaches have their differences, more striking to me are their similarities. The notion that individuals are not a means to an end but rather ends in themselves is fundamental to religious, philosophical, and cultural approaches. The view that human law and natural law are inextricably linked to the common good ties together legal, philosophical, and religious approaches. The sense that fairness is fundamental to ethical behavior appears to be universal.

As noted earlier, however, actually recognizing these ethical boundaries in practice is not always straightforward. How then to operationalize the finding of these lines between the ethical and unethical? A simple starting point is to look at the motivations underlying the activity in question. If the purpose of an activity is to deceive, to cheat others, or to exploit complexity to take advantage of others, then it is surely suspect. Looking at motivation draws on a long history of religious and philosophical precedents, and intentionality also plays an enhanced role in the law. As Oliver Wendell Holmes Jr. noted, "even a dog distinguishes between being stumbled over and being kicked."[22]

In the next four chapters, we head into the "gray" and look at specific examples of market behaviors that appear to fall within these general categories. Our goal is to understand better the nexus of arbitrage and ethics. As we shall see, the complexity of modern finance and modern markets makes this determination challenging.

Into the Gray . . .

CHAPTER 6

ARBITRAGE AND DECEPTION

Oh, what a tangled web we weave / When first we practise to deceive!

—WALTER SCOTT

ARMED WITH THE tools of modern finance, we are ready to transform cash flows in myriad ways. Schooled in the use of arbitrage techniques, we can value a plethora of securities, some natural and others synthetic. Empowered by both knowledge and technology, we can create a vast array of financial contracts. But can we discern when such activities cross the lines of ethical behavior? In this chapter, we return to the central task of this book—determining the linkages between arbitrage and ethics in financial markets.

I suggested earlier that a starting point for such a determination is to look at the motivations behind an activity. Here we begin with what may be the most straightforward case—the use of arbitrage techniques to deceive. We consider three specific examples. First, we examine how Lehman Brothers used repurchase agreements and an accounting trick to make debt "disappear" from its balance sheet. We then look at how Bank of America used mortgage-backed securities to dump "bad" subprime loans onto unsuspecting buyers. Finally, we examine how Goldman Sachs structured a complex financial transaction involving a synthetic collateralized debt obligation to entice investors into a less than transparent investment. Our question in each case: does this cross the lines of ethical behavior?

What Debt?
Lehman Brothers Repo 105

The failure of Lehman Brothers, a major New York investment bank, in September 2008 was a pivotal event in the financial crisis. Lehman Brothers had over $600 billion in assets at the time of its bankruptcy filing, making it the largest bankruptcy in U.S. history. The decision by U.S. regulators to allow Lehman Brothers to fail, rather than to bail it out as they had done for the fellow investment bank Bear Stearns half a year earlier, had cataclysmic effects on the market. Regulators immediately found themselves confronted with a run on institutional money market funds, the imminent failure of the insurance giant AIG, and the potential failures of the investment banks Goldman Sachs and Morgan Stanley as a result of their inability to borrow money in a now frantic market. While the particular timing of Lehman Brothers' demise was a surprise to the market, the fact that the investment bank was in trouble was not. Lehman Brothers, like most investment banks, was involved in a wide range of activities, including the trading of government bonds and other securities, the underwriting of debt and new equity issuances, and the origination and distribution of mortgage-backed securities, often based on subprime loans. Bear Stearns had engaged in a similar set of activities, and its failure (and subsequent regulator-assisted takeover by JPMorgan Chase) in March 2008 clearly signaled potential problems at Lehman Brothers. It added to this concern that Lehman Brothers, in common with most investment banks, relied on large amounts of short-term debt to fund its operations. If Lehman was unable to roll over this outstanding debt, illiquidity would quickly lead to insolvency. Thus, the amount of debt that financed Lehman operations was of great importance to market observers. As a public company, Lehman had to disclose such information on a quarterly basis.

Using some tools of modern finance (along with creative accounting practices and a side trip to London), Lehman Brothers found a way to make some of this debt "disappear" from its balance sheet right before the ends of quarters. To understand exactly what it did, we first have to understand a bit more about its short-term funding needs. As a large investment bank, Lehman had an active trading desk that bought and sold securities for its clients and for its own account. Purchasing securities, as well as holding them in inventory, is expensive, and it requires the firm to commit large amounts of capital. It also entails large amounts of cash, as the firm is required to clear and settle its trades. Large trading banks typically borrow large amounts of very short-term debt, often for maturities as short as one night, to finance these activities. They do so through a financing arrangement called a repurchase agreement. A "repo" facilitates the transformation of an illiquid asset (the security) into a liquid asset (cash).

A repurchase agreement is essentially a short-term loan that is secured by the underlying security holdings. A repo is actually two transactions, because the firm initially sells the security to its counterparty with the simultaneous agreement to buy it back (or repurchase it) the next day (in the case of an overnight repo). Hence, the seller receives cash up front, but must return the cash plus interest (called the repo rate) at the end of the transaction—in effect, using the inventory as collateral for a loan against it. Because there is always some risk between the beginning and end of the transaction, the seller pledges a bit more collateral (say 102 percent of the loan) to protect the lender against the borrower's being unable to return the security. A repo is considered a financing rather than a sale, so both the securities and the repurchase agreement remain on the firm's balance sheet.

Lehman Brothers found a way to get around this balance sheet requirement by using a gambit called Repo 105. The goal of this transaction was to remove both the assets and the financing from the firm's balance sheet. In doing so, Lehman would appear to have less debt, and thus be less leveraged, to an outside observer. Of course, this would be the case only for a few days because Repo 105, like all repos, is a very short-term transaction. But if those few days occurred at the end of financial quarters (when Lehman had to file its 10-Q financial statements), then Lehman would appear healthier than it actually was.[1] And if it did so quarter after quarter, its exact situation would remain obscured.

The actual transaction is complicated only because Lehman had to finagle its way around both accounting and legal rules. No U.S. law firm would countenance the transaction (we have rules against "parking assets" in the United States), so Lehman executed Repo 105 in London. To get around U.S. rules, it essentially created a "synthetic" U.S. repo by executing Repo 105 in London. UK rules allowed the firm to book the transaction as a "sale" rather than as a financing if the amount of collateral pledged was at least 105 percent of the cash it received and the assets received back were "equivalent assets" but not necessarily the same ones. The rules also required that the transaction be done entirely through Lehman's European operation, Lehman Brothers International Europe (LBIE). Figure 7 illustrates the workings of a Repo 105 transaction.

How valuable was this transaction to Lehman Brothers? From a financing perspective, not at all—it was more expensive than a standard repurchase agreement because the firm had to pledge greater collateral as well as to pay the repo rate. But from an optics perspective, this transaction was a gold mine. Lehman did approximately $38.6 billion in the fourth quarter 2007, $49.1 billion in the first quarter 2008, and $50.38 billion in second quarter 2008 in Repo 105 transactions.[2] At a time when the market was concerned about the amount of debt financing the firm, Lehman was removing as much as $50 billion dollars of that debt magically from its balance sheet in the days surrounding its quarter ends (and, of course, putting it back right afterwards). Interestingly, it was not only the market that was misled about Lehman's true leverage position. These transactions were also kept secret from the board of directors, the SEC, the ratings agencies, and even the firm's outside disclosure counsel.[3]

How, then, to view this transaction? Was this ethical behavior? In my view, the answer is no. While apparently not strictly illegal, the careful report of the bankruptcy examiner bringing this transaction to light noted that it "lacked a business purpose."[4] This sentiment was also expressed by Lehman Brothers' controller, Martin Kelly, who believed "the only purpose or motive for the transactions was balance sheet reduction" and felt that there was "no substance to the transactions."[5] Moreover, internal emails offer a similar view: "It's basically window dressing," which elicited the response "I see . . . so it's legally doable but doesn't look good when we do it? Does the rest of the street do

Figure 7
The Mechanics of Repo 105

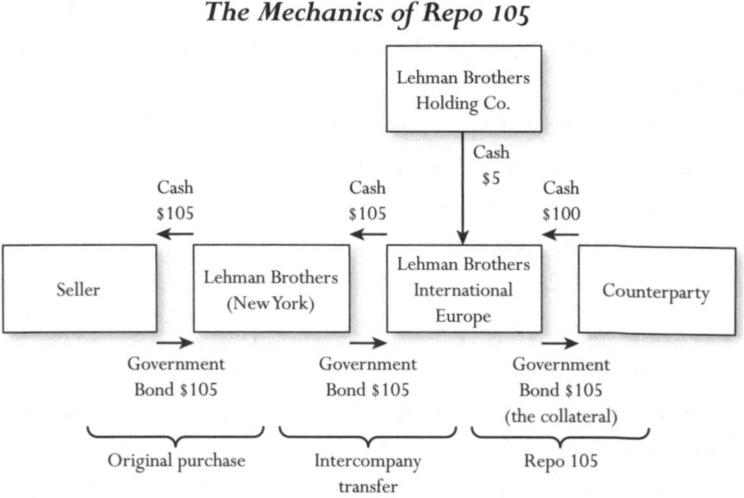

Source: Report of Anton R. Valukas, U.S. Bankruptcy Court, In re Lehman Brothers Holdings, Case 08-13555.

The purpose of this transaction was to remove debt from Lehman's balance sheet. Lehman Brothers (New York) transferred a government bond for $105 to its European arm, Lehman Brothers International Europe. LBIE then entered into a short-term repurchase agreement to sell the bond to a counterparty with the simultaneous agreement to buy it back a few days later. LBIE delivered the bond worth $105 and received $100. LBIE transferred that $100 along with $5 borrowed from the Lehman Brothers Holding Company back to Lehman Brothers New York. Lehman Brothers New York ended up with more cash and less debt on its balance sheet. The entire transaction was then unwound a few days later, as the cash went out and the bond came back.

this?" and the follow-up reply "Yes" and "No." A transaction done only to deceive would surely fail Kant's criterion of doing the right thing for the right reason.

Would it have mattered if the true level of the firm's indebtedness had been known? Certainly, to a creditor lending money to Lehman or to an investor holding Lehman stock the true debt level was important. Had creditors known the true position, they might have demanded higher compensation for lending money to Lehman or, worse still, been unwilling to lend at all. Investors might have perceived the company to be riskier, with a consequent negative impact on its stock price. The board of directors might have made different decisions had it known how precarious the firm's true position actually was. The fact that Lehman's management went to great efforts to hide these positions only reinforces the importance of this information. While these transactions may have furthered the self-interest of the management, the overall consequences of Repo 105 were surely negative. Even Bentham might have objected to this transaction!

Firms always make judgments regarding the correct way to disclose information to the market. Making the firm look as good as possible is not unethical. What is unethical is to purposely misrepresent the firm's position for the purposes of deceiving the market. In the aftermath of Lehman's failure, the Financial Accounting Standards Board changed the rules regarding repurchase agreements to preclude future use of Repo 105 type transactions. In 2013, Ernst & Young, Lehman Brothers accountants, while denying all liability, did agree to pay $99 million to settle claims in an investor class action suit that it, along with Lehman's officers and directors, misled investors about Lehman Brothers' financial condition.[6] While the legal issues here may be in doubt, the ethical ones seem pretty clear.

Securitizing Assets for Fun and Profit—Bank of America and Mortgage-Backed Securities

In August 2014, the Department of Justice announced a historic settlement with Bank of America—an astonishing $16.65 billion in fines and required payouts. Described as "the largest civil settlement with a single entity in American history," the settlement resolved a wide range of federal and state claims against Bank of America and its subsidiaries Merrill Lynch and Countrywide Financial, relating to the sale of mortgages and mortgaged-backed securities. The DOJ noted that "the significance of this settlement lies not just in its size; this agreement is notable because it achieves real accountability for the American people and helps to rectify the harm caused by Bank of America's conduct. . . ."[7] The actual misconduct involves a wide range of activities, far too numerous to be detailed here. Underlying all of them, however, is a common theme: Bank of America and its entities knowingly sold and securitized mortgages that they knew were substandard without disclosing this information to investors. In short, they dumped bad loans on the market.

Some of the ethical issues here are straightforward. For example, Bank of America lied about the quality of the mortgages it delivered to Fannie Mae and Freddie Mac. Explicitly lying is fraud, and it is wrong under any ethical framework. But other issues are more nuanced. Is it ethical to sell to the market mortgages or securities the bank would not be willing to hold on its own balance sheet? What is it about market transactions that encouraged employees to look the other way when it came to selling bad assets? Did these banks actually encourage unethical behavior through their lending processes and compensation packages?

To understand these issues, it is useful to recall our discussion in chapter 3 about mortgage-backed securities. As is depicted in Figure 3, MBSs are formed by pooling residential mortgage loans and then selling bonds based on the mortgages to investors. The underlying mortgages provide the cash flow that will go to the bondholders. These bonds have different pieces, or tranches, structured to meet the needs of specific clients. Thus, from the same underlying collateral, there can be short-term tranches, long-term tranches, tranches that feature fixed interest rates, tranches with floating rates, even tranches with rates that float up when market rates float down. Thanks to the tools of modern finance, the underlying cash flows can be turned into a cornucopia of securities.

This securitization process can be very beneficial: investors have access to new asset classes with securities tailored to their investment needs, while banks and mortgage originators get new funding sources, allowing them to make more mortgage loans to home buyers. But this process is also opaque, because investors know nothing about individual borrowers and borrowers know nothing about who is actually funding their loan. This impersonality can obscure the fact that someone somewhere is actually on the other side of the transaction. This opaqueness also means that underwriters, and credit rating agencies, play a crucial role in ensuring the trustworthiness both of the underlying cash flows and of the securities being created and traded.

Bank of America, Merrill Lynch, and Countrywide Financial were the largest issuers of private mortgage securities in the period 2004–08, together issuing $965 billion in MBSs.[8] Countrywide was by far the most active issuer, accounting for almost three quarters of this total amount. Of these MBSs, $245 billion worth would either default or become severely delinquent; Countrywide was again responsible for issuing the bulk of these bad mortgage securities. Bank of America originated only 4 percent of these impaired securities. During that period, the three companies were separate entities, but the onset of the financial crisis brought severe challenges to both Countrywide and Merrill Lynch. Bank of America purchased Countrywide Financial for $4 billion in January 2008, and it agreed to buy Merrill Lynch for $50 billion on September 14, 2008. Both transactions were viewed at the time as rescuing firms that were in danger of failing.

The allegations against Merrill Lynch involved seventy-two MBSs composed of residential subprime mortgages. Merrill Lynch, as an investment bank, underwrote or issued MBSs by purchasing the underlying mortgages from so-called third-party originators (essentially firms specializing in originating mortgages) and then structuring the MBS securities and selling them to investors. In issuing these MBSs, Merrill made representations to the SEC, the credit ratings agencies, and the investors in these products as to the underwriting guidelines surrounding the underlying loans. These guidelines involved factors such as the income level, employment status, and other characteristics of the borrowers, as well as the loan-to-value ratio and other characteristics of the mortgage. On the basis of these representations, the credit rating agencies rated the tranches in the MBSs, and investors relied on those ratings in their investment decisions.

Prior to including any loan in a mortgage pool, Merrill conducted internal due diligence on the loans. Exceptions to underwriting and other compliance guidelines were noted, and these loans were then flagged for additional interval review. Here the process appeared to falter—up to 50 percent of some loan pools were flagged as noncompliant, but were often waived into the MBSs anyway. This led one consultant in Merrill's due diligence department to write, "How much time do you want me to spend going over these loans if [the co-head of Merrill Lynch's RMBS business] is going to keep them regardless of issues? . . . Makes you wonder why we have due diligence performed other than making sure the loan closed."[9] Thus, Merrill Lynch knew that many of the loans being included in its MBS offerings were deficient, but never disclosed this information.

Countrywide also issued MBSs, but as a mortgage lender it originated mortgages both to securitize and to hold as investments on its balance sheet. Countrywide pursued a "supermarket strategy" of providing mortgage products across the spectrum of borrowers, with a particular focus on those needing very large loans and on riskier subprime, Alt-A, and so-called Extreme Alt-A borrowers.[10] Countrywide also specialized in more exotic mortgage loans, such as pay-option adjustable-rate mortgage (ARM) loans. These loans gave borrowers the option to pay less than the interest that accrued on the principal balance, meaning that over time the principal balance grew larger and larger (and the loan grew riskier and riskier).

Over the period 2005–07, the DOJ complaint noted, Countrywide began to see ominous signs that many of the mortgages it originated were performing badly. More than 70 percent of the pay-option ARMs, for example, were paying less than the full interest amount, and Countrywide's own models predicted that defaults in the Extreme Alt-A program could reach "the high 30's or low 40's, and even a few in the 50's." Observing that the Extreme Alt-A loans were a "hazardous product," a Countrywide executive in April 2006 asked "to see a detailed implementation plan which addresses the process for originating and selling these loans such that we are not left with credit risk."[11]

Similarly, recognizing the potential for "both financial and reputational catastrophe," the chairman of Countrywide Financial wrote in August 2005, "I am becoming increasingly concerned about the environment surrounding the borrowers who are utilizing the pay option loan. . . . We must therefore re-think what assets [we] should be putting in the bank."[12] By September 2006, the chairman sent a more explicit memo: "The bottom line is we are flying blind on how these loans will perform in a stressed environment of higher unemployment, reduced value and slowing home sales. . . . I believe the timing is right for us to sell all newly originated pay options and begin rolling off the bank balance sheet, in an orderly manner, pay options currently on their portfolio."[13]

Notice what is not being said here: the bank is not going to stop originating such loans. Instead, the strategy switches to originating them and then immediately selling the loans outright or via securitization to somebody else. The implications of such a strategy were not lost on Countrywide's executives. Its president in 2005 warned of "securitization implications" and wrote, "We need to analyze what remains if the bank is only cherry picking and what remains to be securitized/sold is overly concentrated with higher risk loans. . . . [T]he remaining production then increasingly looks like an adversely selected pool."[14]

As we discussed in chapter 5, such adverse selection can ultimately lead to market failure. But, of course, that occurs only when the participants in the market realize that the assets they are buying are "lemons." However, Countrywide, like Merrill Lynch, did not disclose such information to the market. Indeed, freed from the constraint that it might actually have to suffer losses on the loans it originated, Countrywide originated more and more loans, many in violation of the company's underwriting norms. As one memo directed, Countrywide should "take advantage of the 'salability' and do loans outside guidelines and not let our views of risk get in the way."[15] This behavior, in turn, meant that adverse selection in the securitized products became even greater. The eventual collapse of the private MBS market during the financial crisis was only a matter of time.

What, then, to make of the ethical implications of this behavior? One could argue that markets are markets: that "buyer beware" should govern the purchase of any sophisticated financial product. Moreover, since the credit ratings agencies gave these products high marks, it was not up to the underwriters to tell the credit raters how to do their jobs. (Clearly, though, someone should have told them because the credit ratings ultimately proved wildly deficient.) Yet, such temporizing misses the basic point that markets rely on fair dealing and trust to operate. Knowing that the mortgage loans were of much lower quality than was depicted in their disclosures, and selling them anyway, is unethical. Certainly, it fails the "do unto others as you would have them do unto you" standard—Countrywide would never have bought the mortgages that it was busy dumping on someone else. But it also fails even the basic ethical standards of the consequential approach—selling these loans to someone else did not make the loans any better; it simply meant that someone else would bear the loss. And by its packaging up of massive numbers of these loans the entire market ultimately failed. The cost-benefit calculus does not seem even close!

Is the problem here with markets, with selling securities to others you would not want to hold on your own balance sheet? My answer to this specific question is no, and the reason why goes to the heart of what is wrong here. Markets are very good at trading things, even things with very disparate quality levels. To understand why, consider a more familiar analogy—betting on football games. Suppose that the New England Patriots are playing the Tennessee Titans. Since New England almost always wins and Tennessee almost always loses, this would not seem like a very good bet; everyone will want to be on the same side. But would the bet be so lopsided if Tennessee had to lose by more than 15 points? Now we have a more interesting wager, and the point spread will adjust until the amount bet on New England equals the amount bet on Tennessee. This is what also happens in markets. Buyers and sellers can disagree on what something is worth, and a market price will emerge to balance those willing to sell with those willing to buy. Of course, betting markets and trading markets work only if buyers and sellers have enough information to evaluate the transaction.

Returning to the case at hand, if the market had sufficient information about the mortgages' true quality, then a fair exchange would have been possible. In that case, the market price of those mortgage loans would have been much lower, and Countrywide's choice between keeping them on the balance sheet or securitizing them would have been based on issues other than risk. Of course, had the quality been clearer, the credit rating agencies would not have given the securities the same ratings, deterring many would-be MBS purchasers. And, without a market in which to sell these mortgages, Countrywide would have made fewer of them in the first place. The linkages in modern financial markets are long and complex.

Why did the bankers at Merrill Lynch and Countrywide Financial think it acceptable to sell loans to others that they clearly knew were "bad"? One argument, put forth by Judge Richard Posner, is that banking simply attracts the wrong sort of people. In a blog post entitled "Is Banking Unusually Corrupt, and If So, Why?," Posner paints a bleak picture of banking, one in which, left unsupervised, the banking industry "becomes a Darwinian jungle, with bankers as predators and their customers (and each other) as prey."[16] What causes this outcome? Posner argues,

> Any firm that has short-term capital is under great pressure to compete ferociously, as it is in constant danger of losing its capital to fiercer, less scrupulous competitors, who can offer its investors and its key employees higher returns.
>
> Such a business model attracts people who have a taste for risk and attach a very high utility to money. The complexity of modern finance, the greed and gullibility of individual financial consumers, and the difficulty that so many ordinary people have in understanding credit facilitate financial fraud, and financial sharp practices that fall short of fraud, enabling financial fraudsters to skirt criminal sanctions.[17]

The "financial fraudster" theory can be made to fit the "facts," but is that really what is going on? I don't think so. Instead, I find that insights from the field of behavioral ethics provide a more compelling explanation. Behavioral ethics argues that a variety of cognitive biases can lead good people to act unethically without their own awareness. One such bias is "motivated blindness," or the psychological tendency of people to see what they want to see and miss contradictory information when it is in their interest to remain ignorant. Another bias is that the more indirect the harm, the less real it seems to decision-makers. Thus, "statistical" victims do not elicit the sympathy attaching to identifiable victims, and so are much more easily overlooked.

Max Bazerman and Ann Tenbrunsel, in their article "Ethical Breakdowns," point to design issues in the Ford Pinto (engineers knew that its gas tanks could rupture but went ahead into production anyway) as an example of these effects.[18] Why did they produce a car that they knew was defective? A focus on meeting deadlines, an unwillingness to convey bad news to higher-ups, compensation schemes that reward completing tasks on time—all can contribute to "blindness" when it comes to ethical issues. The fact that someone somewhere would be hurt when the gas tank exploded was relegated to a nebulous "cost" of production.

The situation at Countrywide seems remarkably similar to that at Ford. In separate litigation that was recently overturned on appeal, the government charged Countrywide with defrauding Fannie Mae and Freddie Mac by selling them bad loans generated through the bank's High Speed Swim Lane, or "Hustle," program. The government alleged that the program compensated employees according to the number of mortgages produced, removed financial penalties that previously attached to making bad loans, and excluded underwriters from the loan approval process in favor of automated processing. Moreover, the court found that the head of the Hustle program "scathingly denounced those who raised concerns."[19] With such an incentive structure, it is little wonder that a program designed to churn out mortgages with scant regard for quality created a lot of bad loans! For Countrywide, as for Ford, motivating people to ignore ethics seems to yield bad outcomes, regardless of the industry.[20]

You Should Have Asked—Goldman Sachs and the Abacus Deal

In April 2010, the Securities and Exchange Commission (SEC) dropped a bombshell on the market by announcing that it was suing Goldman Sachs for fraud in connection with its structuring and marketing of a subprime mortgage-related securities deal named Abacus 207-AC1. The SEC alleged that Goldman defrauded investors by misstating and omitting key facts related to the complex synthetic consolidated debt obligation. In the words of Robert Khuzami, the SEC's director of enforcement, "The product is new and complex, but the deception and conflicts are old and simple."[21]

The ethical issues surrounding the Abacus deal are complex. Did Goldman Sachs intentionally defraud customers? Since the customers involved were all seemingly sophisticated financial institutions, was Goldman under any obligation to tell them about every aspect of the deal, or should they have known to ask? Did the complexity of this financial product allow Goldman to mislead otherwise knowledgeable investors? When does a "deal" cross the line from being a market transaction with winners and losers to being an unethical venture designed to exploit investors?

To understand even the mechanics of the Abacus deal is a non-trivial undertaking, to say nothing of then discerning its ethical status! Abacus is a synthetic consolidated debt obligation based on residential subprime mortgage-backed securities. In chapter 3, we discussed mortgage-backed securities, credit default swaps, and synthetic securities, all of which come into play in this transaction. But as we also discussed, modern finance is really about packaging cash flows to create the securities that clients want. What did clients think they were getting from participating in this specific transaction? Since multiple clients were involved, the answer to this question is not straightforward.

The Abacus deal was structured and sold to clients late 2007. At that time, problems in the housing market (particularly the subprime segment) were emerging, but the situation was not yet viewed, at least by the ratings agencies, as a crisis. Consequently, mortgaged-backed bonds were still garnering AAA ratings, and borrowers around the world were purchasing tranches of those bonds as safe, but slightly higher-yielding, alternatives to more standard fixed-income investments. Indeed, the demand for such investments, particularly for the even higher yields that attached to securities based on subprime mortgages, far outstripped the supply. With the "natural" supply limited by the availability of subprime mortgages to serve as collateral, Goldman Sachs and other Wall Street firms turned to creating synthetic versions known as synthetic collateralized debt obligations.[22]

A synthetic CDO is constructed with credit default swaps (CDS). As with other synthetic securities, there is a reference asset (in this case, a portfolio of residential mortgage-backed securities), and the CDS is written against this reference asset. Despite the name, recall that a CDS is not a swap but a type of put option. If there is a credit event (i.e., a default or a downgrade), the writer of the CDS must make a payment to the buyer of the CDS. In return for this protection, the CDS writer receives a yearly premium from the CDS buyer. Because CDS writers bear the risk of the underlying asset and receive the yearly premium, their position is essentially the same as that of owning the natural CDO.

The Abacus deal was originated to meet the needs of a specific client, Jon Paulson. Paulson ran a large and successful hedge fund, and he wished to make a bet against the subprime mortgage market. One way to do so is to buy a CDS on a portfolio of subprime mortgage-backed securities. CDSs are often used by holders of securities to provide "insurance" on their portfolios; if a credit event occurs and the security loses value, then the payoff to the CDS hedges the loss. If you do not own the underlying securities, however, then buying a CDS is akin to taking a "short" position on the portfolio—you "win" if the securities go down in value and the CDS pays off. Paulson believed that this would be the case in the subprime mortgage market, and so he approached Goldman Sachs to create such a security.

The structure of the Abacus deal is depicted in Figure 8. Paulson gave Goldman a list of ninety residential mortgage-backed securities (RMBS) that he wanted to be the reference assets for the deal. These particular RMBS were based on mortgage loans made in hard-hit locales such as California and Nevada, and in

Figure 8

The Abacus Deal—A Synthetic CDO

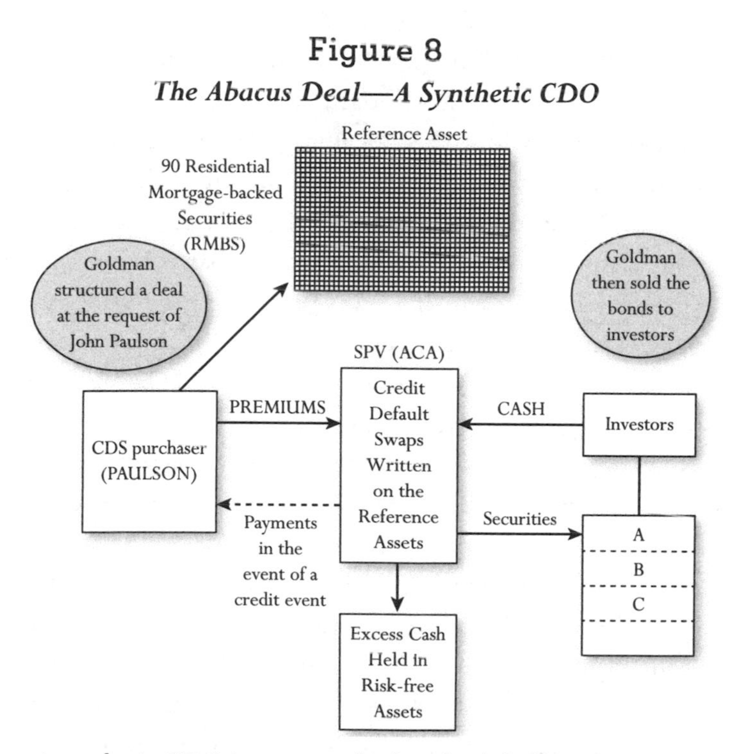

A synthetic CDO is composed of credit default swaps written on a portfolio of reference assets composed of mortgage-backed securities. The writer of the CDS bears the exposure to the default risk of the reference assets and is paid a premium for bearing this risk. The premiums are held in risk-free assets so that the synthetic CDO has the same exposure as a CDO constructed from the reference assets. Investors are then sold bonds on the basis of the returns to the underlying credit default swaps.

Paulson's view they were highly likely to be downgraded. Goldman asked the firm ACA, a structurer (or manager) of synthetic CDOs, to create such a security, and then sent it the list of underlying securities to be used for the reference asset. Notable here is that Goldman did not reveal to ACA the particular role played by Paulson.

The synthetic CDO in this deal would have as its collateral the CDS written on these reference assets, with bonds sold to investors on the basis of this collateral. The cash flow to these bond investors would come from the premiums paid by the CDS buyers, and from interest earned on the reinvestment of these premiums in safe assets. Investors in the Abacus bonds would lose money to the extent there were payoffs of the CDS owing to credit events. Paulson bought all of the CDS. He would make money if the reference RMBS were downgraded (and hence the CDSs paid off), and he would lose money otherwise. Goldman Sachs, acting as the underwriter, sold the Synthetic CDO Abacus bonds to institutional investors. According to the SEC complaint, Paulson & Co. paid Goldman Sachs approximately $15 million dollars for structuring and marketing Abacus.[23]

It was not long before problems surfaced in the reference portfolio. The Abacus 2007-AC1 deal issued on April 26, 2007, and by October 24, 2007, 83 percent of the underlying RMBS bonds had been downgraded. By February 2008, 100 percent% of the RMBS in the reference portfolio had been downgraded.[24] Paulson & Co. made a profit of $1 billion, while the holders of the Abacus bonds lost a similar amount. The SEC would file its complaint against Goldman alleging fraud a little over two years later.

The SEC alleged that Goldman structured an investment that it knew was "designed to fail" and sold that security to its clients, who then lost hundreds of millions of dollars.[25] The complaint held that Goldman knew it could not sell the bonds connected with this transaction without the participation of an objective portfolio selection agent (in this case ACA) and that Goldman deceived ACA with respect to the role played by Paulson. ACA actually lost substantial sums of money in this deal, in part because it believed that Paulson was taking a long position (i.e., betting on the underlying assets to do well) and that his interests would thus be aligned with those of the Abacus bondholders. The opposite was, of course, true—Paulson was betting against the underlying assets. Goldman "did not disclose Paulson & Co.'s short position or its role in the collateral selection process in the term sheet, flip book, offering memorandum, or other marketing materials provided to investors."[26]

Goldman argued strenuously that it did not commit fraud. Viewing the case from its perspective, one could counter that Goldman did not deceive ACA—that if ACA did not understand the role played by Paulson it should have asked. Moreover, this deal was sold only to institutional investors who could have, and should have, understood the risks of such a transaction. The nature of a synthetic CDO requires that somewhere there is someone buying the CDS, in effect taking the opposite side of the trade. These clients should have also understood that Goldman did proprietary trading (i.e., it traded for its own account) and that it sometimes took positions in the transactions it structured. Goldman was not under any obligation to ensure that its clients' interests and Goldman's aligned.

The regulatory side of this case ended on July 16, 2008, when Goldman Sachs agreed to settle civil charges by paying a $550 million fine to the SEC. As part of the settlement, Goldman issued the following statement:

> Goldman acknowledges that the marketing materials for the ABACUS 2007- AC1 transaction contained incomplete information. In particular, it was a mistake for the Goldman marketing materials to state that the reference portfolio was "selected by" ACA Management LLC without disclosing the role of Paulson & Co. Inc. in the portfolio selection process and that Paulson's economic interests were adverse to CDO investors. Goldman regrets that the marketing materials did not contain that disclosure.[27]

The SEC declared that the accord is "a stark lesson to Wall Street firms that no product is too complex, and no investor too sophisticated, to avoid a heavy price if a firm violates the fundamental principles of honest treatment and fair dealing." The $550 million fine was the largest ever assessed by the SEC against a single Wall Street firm. Yet, while substantial, the fine represented just fourteen days of Goldman's first-quarter profits in 2010, prompting some to term the settlement a "steal" for Goldman.[28] Who actually "won" or "lost" the legal tussle between the SEC and Goldman Sachs remains a subject of debate.

More germane for our purposes is a different question: did this transaction cross the lines of ethical behavior? At some level, one could argue that Goldman simply used the tools of modern finance to meet the needs of its clients. For Jon Paulson, those needs entailed designing a transaction that allowed him to bet against the housing market. Indeed, one way to view Paulson's transaction was as a form of "ratings arbitrage" in that he believed the models Moody's and other credit rating agencies were using to give RMBS AAA ratings were flawed and that they did not reflect the realities of the underlying subprime market.[29] By using the tools of modern finance, he could profit when the errors in those models were revealed. Similarly, the investors who bought the Abacus bonds were seeking structured products that could provide expected returns in excess of what was available from existing fixed-income products. Creating a synthetic CDO offered a way to give these investors access to otherwise unavailable investment opportunities.

Yet, the difficulty with this analysis is that it ignores the fact that the needs of the two groups were diametrically opposed. Goldman's internal emails suggest the firm was well aware of this conflict, describing the Abacus deal as "complex, highly leveraged, exotic trades" that were "monstrosities!!!" created "without necessarily understanding all of the implications" of the transactions, and describing the arrangement between Goldman and Paulson as "surreal." Other emails noted, "The cdo biz is dead we don't have a lot of time left."[30]

Goldman's decision not to disclose the role played by Paulson and Co. to the other participants in the transaction, or to ACA, which was managing the deal, amounted, in my view, to deception. The SEC would argue that failing to disclose violated the norms of "honest treatment and fair dealing," an outcome surely at variance with ethical behavior. But the issues here are not simply legal. If Goldman had revealed the role played by Paulson in the selection of the securities, would the same outcome have prevailed? Would anyone have been willing to invest in a deal that was designed to fail? By neglecting to disclose, Goldman was not "dealing justly," a criterion at least Aristotle would argue is needed for ethical behavior. Moreover, since Goldman earned $15 million in fees from Paulson, choosing to hide this connection essentially meant that Goldman put its needs ahead of those of its other clients. Self-interest has a way of obscuring the existence of ethical dilemmas.

Another factor obscuring ethical dilemmas is what behavioral researchers call the omission bias. The omission bias is the implicit belief that harm done by action (or commission) is morally worse than equivalent harm done by inaction (or omission).[31] Thus, explicitly lying to a client who then suffers a loss would be unethical, but not telling the client something that results in the same loss is not so bad. If you are the client, it is not clear you see much difference in moral culpability.

CHAPTER 7

ARBITRAGING REGULATORY AND MARKET STRUCTURES

Know the rules well,
so you can break them effectively.

—DALAI LAMA XIV

ARBITRAGE CAN BE used to exploit rigidities arising in many cases from regulation. By removing inefficiencies, regulatory arbitrage can improve the functioning of markets, lower the costs of transacting, and allow new, less expensive synthetic versions of financial products to emerge. But regulatory arbitrage can also have a "dark" side in that it can be used to essentially gut rules and regulations, as well as to exploit other participants in a market.

In this chapter, we consider how such arbitrage-based activities can cross the lines of ethical behavior. I provide one (perhaps surprising) good example of regulatory arbitrage—Bernie

Madoff and the Cincinnati Stock Exchange—and two (less surprising) bad examples—JPMorgan Chase and the California electricity market and Goldman Sachs and the aluminum market. In the JPMorgan case, the question is when does arbitrage behavior cross the line from ameliorating market inefficiencies to manipulating markets? In the Goldman case, the focus is more on the ethics of commercial transactions—how far can you go in exploiting customers and markets? As we shall see, discerning the linkages between arbitrage and ethics is not always straightforward.

Bernie Madoff and the Cincinnati Stock Exchange

Few names are more identified with reprehensible behavior than that of Bernie Madoff. The Ponzi scheme that defrauded thousands of investors, embarrassed scores of regulators, and landed Madoff in jail for a staggering 150-year sentence was front-page news around the world. Less well known is that Bernie Madoff, in earlier times, was instrumental in changing the way stock trading worked for individual, or "retail," traders. As *Traders Magazine* noted, he "almost single-handedly created the modern-day Third Market for retail orders."[1] He did so by arbitraging the rules that defined where orders had to execute in the stock market.

Stocks today trade in a multitude of settings, but that was not always the case. Prior to the development of Nasdaq in 1971, stocks traded on the New York Stock Exchange (NYSE), on a handful of regional stock exchanges, and in the dispersed over-the-counter market. The introduction of an electronic quote display system (Nasdaq is the acronym for the National Association of Securities Dealers automated quotation system) allowed smaller dealers to compete for order flow, and Bernard L. Madoff

Investment Securities (BMIS) was one of approximately five hundred such dealer firms quoting on the system. The bulk of trading volume, however, was in NYSE-listed stocks, and these stocks traded almost exclusively on the NYSE. In part, this was because of regulations such as NYSE Rule 390, which prohibited NYSE member firms from executing particular NYSE-listed stocks away from the floor of the exchange.[2]

Two trends, however, signaled changes ahead. One was technology, which allowed for greater automation in the processing and execution of trades. The second was a new regulatory environment that favored the development of more competition. The launch of the Intermarket Trading System (ITS) in 1978, which electronically linked the regional exchanges and the NYSE via a consolidated tape showing quotes and trades, set the stage for a national market system to emerge. This, in turn, let market makers on regional exchanges compete for order flow with the NYSE by posting quotes on the ITS. The ITS also allowed determination of the best bid or offer across markets, known as the National Best Bid and Offer (NBBO).

Bernie Madoff positioned his firm to capitalize on these developments by investing heavily in new technology. By 1988, his trading systems could electronically receive incoming orders, automatically fill orders up to three thousand shares at the NBBO, and do so in less than ten seconds.[3] Since the NYSE took up to ninety seconds to report back on trades, BMIS was the high-frequency trader of its day. BMIS also became a member firm of the Cincinnati Stock Exchange (CSE), one of the many regional exchanges linked by the ITS. The CSE dated back to 1885, but its adoption in 1980 of an electronic trading platform made it the country's first electronic stock exchange.[4] As a CSE market maker, BMIS could directly compete with the NYSE.

Market makers provide liquidity in markets by being willing to buy and sell a security. The NYSE executed the vast majority of trade in its listed stocks, and the liquidity available on the exchange floor made it a magnet for order flow. This concentration of liquidity, in turn, made it easier for the NYSE market makers (called specialists) to quote the best prices to buy and sell the stock. In the world of stock trading, the conventional wisdom was that liquidity begat liquidity. So, taking on New York was a tall order.

Bernie Madoff saw an opportunity, however, in retail order flow—the orders submitted by individual investors to their brokerage accounts at firms like Charles Schwab or Fidelity. Retail order flow was attractive for a variety of reasons. The large retail brokerage houses could link directly with BMIS, providing a conduit for these orders to electronically route to the Madoff market-making operation. It was equally important that, unlike institutional traders who may be trading on new information, retail traders are typically "uninformed" in the sense that their orders do not generally portend future movements in stock prices. Because market making involves buying when traders are selling, and selling when traders are buying, the market maker loses to informed traders.

There is a large body of research analyzing how these trader clienteles affect price setting in markets. Much like the MBS investors mentioned in the preceding chapter who got only the loans Countrywide didn't want, market makers face an adverse selection problem if they trade with too many informed traders. To balance these potential losses, market makers must have gains from trading with the uninformed traders. This is accomplished by setting a spread between the price at which the market maker will buy the security (the bid price) and the price at which the market maker will sell the security (the ask price). The spread, the difference between the bid and ask prices, balances the adverse selection problem the market maker faces.

Spreads are also affected by regulation, particularly by rules setting minimum spread sizes. The minimum spread now is only a penny, but in Bernie Madoff's time it was an eighth, or 12.5 cents. For a smaller stock, this was not an issue, as it typically traded with a larger spread. But for the largest, liquid stocks trading on the NYSE, spreads were typically at this minimum "one tick." In the view of many market participants, the minimum for these stocks was too large.

Bernie Madoff set out to capture the retail market by offering the large brokerage houses an intriguing deal—send their retail orders up to three thousand shares in the 250 largest stocks to BMIS. BMIS would automatically execute these orders on the Cincinnati Stock Exchange at the prevailing bid or ask on the NYSE (or at a better price if New York was not quoting the best price). He would know what these prices were because they were disseminated over the Intermarket Trading System consolidated quote feed that determined the national best bid or offer. He would do it faster than the NYSE, and charge no exchange fee. To sweeten the deal, BMIS would also pay the broker a penny per share in each order.

The economics here are intriguing. The brokers saved on execution costs and got payment for order flow. The retail traders got the same price they would have gotten had the order gone to the NYSE. And Bernie Madoff got massive numbers of retail orders, taking him from doing 2 percent of the volume in NYSE-listed stocks in 1989 to 9 percent in 1992. A win, win, win so to speak! Of course, as in many arbitrages, there can be a loser, and in this case it was the NYSE. Orders that would have gone to the NYSE were diverted instead to Cincinnati.

Why was this working? Bernie Madoff essentially created a synthetic NYSE trade for retail investors by arbitraging regulatory rigidities. The key here is the spread. Technology (i.e., the ITS display of the NYSE quotes) allowed BMIS to match these spreads, in effect free riding on the price discovery process taking place at the NYSE. But Madoff was not dealing with the same order flow as the NYSE, because he accepted only the "uninformed" retail trade. Spreads for these orders should have been smaller because they had lower adverse selection.[5] So BMIS could actually rebate part of these spreads to the traders and still make a great profit. The minimum tick size exacerbated this problem by artificially keeping spreads high. The NYSE could not copy what Bernie Madoff was doing because by law an exchange, unlike a broker, must accept all orders sent to it.

A simple analogy can make this clearer. Think of the order flow like individuals in a group health insurance plan. Some people are healthier than others, and so consume less medical care. Other people are sicker, and require costly care. A group health insurance plan charges a single premium, in effect having healthy people subsidize the sicker ones. Suppose now another insurer makes this offer to the healthy people: come to my plan, and I will match the coverage and the premiums you are paying on your old plan, plus give you a rebate. For the healthy people, this seems like a no-brainer. But notice its implications for the sicker people: once the healthy folks are gone, the premium must increase to cover the greater proportion of sick people in the pool. In effect, the adverse selection in the pool has increased. With the new plan matching the premiums of the old plan, the new plan can now also raise premiums, allowing it to rebate even more money.

Returning to the issue at hand, was Bernie Madoff's strategy unethical? In my view, no. Madoff exploited market rigidities resulting from fixed minimum spreads and "one size fits all" pricing in exchanges. He found a way to make retail traders (and their brokers) better-off by segmenting the market. This reduced the market share (and profits) the NYSE had enjoyed from trading these securities. He broke no laws or market regulations in making the markets more competitive, which was the goal of the SEC in implementing the ITS system in the first place. He also set in motion many of the changes that would alter securities trading in the coming decades. Arbitrage often creates winners and losers, but that does not mean it is unethical.

Many of the issues raised here continue to dominate discussions of market structure today. Is it fair for trading venues to "free ride" on the price discovery of exchanges? Should payment for order flow be allowed? Should trading be permitted to fragment, or are markets "better" when trading is consolidated? How large should the minimum tick size be in markets? Like Bernie Madoff in the 1980s, we are still looking for answers.

JPMorgan Chase and the California Electricity Market

On July 30, 2013, JPMorgan Chase (JPMC), while neither denying nor admitting the violations, agreed to pay $410 million to the Federal Energy Regulatory Commission (FERC) to settle allegations that the bank's energy traders had manipulated electricity markets in California and the Midwest. The problem here involves what FERC, and the California energy regulator California Independent System Operator (CAISO), described as "manipulative bidding strategies" designed to take advantage of the computerized algorithms allocating production awards to power producers.

The issues here are both complex and intriguing. JPMorgan Chase agreed that it pursued the particular strategies in question, but argued it did not break any rules by exploiting loopholes in power markets.[6] FERC agreed that JPMC's actual bid prices all fell within the allowable range as set by CAISO, but argued that such strategies "were not grounded in the normal forces of supply and demand" but instead were designed "to create artificial conditions that would cause the CAISO system to pay [JPMorgan] outside the market at premium rates."[7] When does arbitraging a system to exploit inefficiencies cross the line into market manipulation? And, even if it is legal, is such behavior ethical?

To understand what JPMC did, we first have to understand the rather arcane world of electricity generation, distribution, and pricing. Electricity is a commodity (energy) with the unique property that it cannot be stored. As illustrated in Figure 9, the electricity market has three pieces, corresponding to the production of electricity by power generating plants, the transmission of the electricity via the power grid, and the eventual delivery of electricity to end users such as firms and consumers. The "wholesale" market involves the production and transmission pieces, while the "retail" market involves its sale to the actual end users. The issues here arise in the wholesale market, but ultimately the costs established there affect the retail market.

JPMC entered the electricity power markets in 2008 via its

Figure 9

Overview of Electricity Generation and Distribution Process

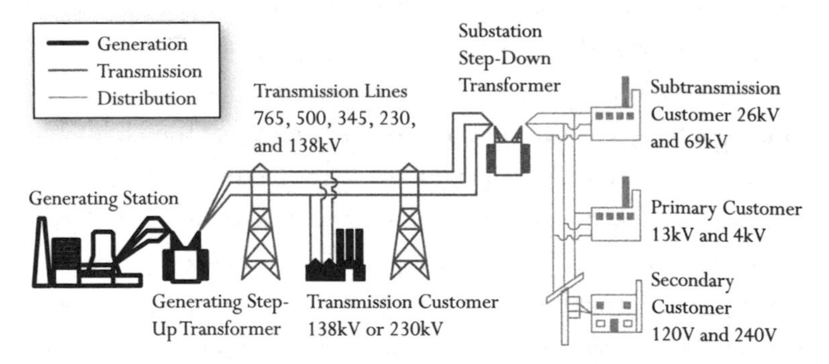

Source: Federal Energy Regulatory Commission website, http://www.asce.org/uploadedFiles/Infrastructure/Failure_to_Act/SCE41%20report_Final-lores.pdf.

acquisition of the troubled investment bank Bear Stearns during the financial crisis. Bear Stearns' energy subsidiary, Bear Energy LP, owned (or had agreements to sell power with) twenty-seven power plants, and these assets were transferred to JPMorgan Chase's energy subsidiary JPMorgan Ventures Energy Corporation. JPMVEC would also add agreements with other power plants, bringing its full or partial ownership stake by 2010 to thirty-one power plants. Several of these power plants were in California, and they are the focus of the discussion here.

Electricity trades like any other commodity in both physical and financial trading venues.[8] The physical wholesale market for electricity has two pieces: the "day-ahead" market and the "real-time" market. Because of the inability to store electricity, the day-ahead market is a forward-looking market producing binding schedules for the production and wholesale purchase of electricity the next day.[9] The real-time market operates to fill the gap between what has been contracted for in the day-ahead market and what is actually demanded by end users during the day. The real-time market is much smaller than the day-ahead market, accounting for only about 5 percent of scheduled energy use. These markets are operated on a state or regional basis by various independent, nonprofit organizations (such as CAISO) to "ensure reliability and optimize supply and demand bids for wholesale electric power."[10] The sellers in these markets are power producers, and the buyers are distributors.

Electrical power plants offer to sell electricity in both physical markets. Because actual demand is volatile and unknown in advance, the market operators (known generically as ISOs) must be ready to meet unexpected demand with little notice. To do so, they can draw on a wide range of power plants, some more efficient than others. Power plants differ in their costs of producing electricity, so when less efficient plants are drawn into production, a variety of special payments are made to cover their costs. Power plants also take time to "ramp up" and "ramp down" to produce electricity, so there are also payments to compensate for these minimum run time expenses as well.

The day-ahead and real-time markets operate as auctions where electricity producers bid to provide units of power measured in megawatts per hour (MWh). The rules of these auctions are remarkably complex. Bidders in the day-ahead market specify both a price for providing power at the unit's lowest operating level (called Pmin) and a price for producing electricity above that level. It is the blended two prices that are used to determine winners in the auction. The bid also specifies the total quantity the producer wishes to sell. Under CAISO rules, the unit can specify its Pmin at two times its actual operating costs, so, for example, a plant that can produce 100 MWh for $4,500 can specify its Pmin as $9,000. The price bid for selling electricity above that amount can range from –$30.00 per MWh upward. A negative price may seem odd, but it is allowed by FERC rules because some producers, such as wind farms, receive tax credits to produce that are larger than their negative bid.[11]

CAISO provides the power seller with an "award" if the ISO agrees to buy power from the seller. The actual price determined in the day-ahead auction is the marginal price that equates the supply and demand in the auction, and it is this price (not the bid price) that is specified in the award. Over the time period in question, this price was typically in the $30–$35 per MWh range. The price the seller actually gets can be greater than this if its production costs qualify for a wide variety of compensatory payments, some of which are discussed shortly.

The real-time market operates the next day. Even if the seller received an award in the day-ahead market, it may not need to produce all the energy called for in the award. "If the ISO does not, in the end, instruct the generator to produce all of the energy specified in the award, the generator can 'buy back' the unneeded portion of the award in the Real Time market."[12] The awardee is guaranteed to sell, however, at least its Pmin quantity, and in doing so it will receive an extra payment to recover its Pmin cost level (i.e., it will get a bid recovery payment of $9,000 for the 100 MKw).

The power plants that JPMC operated in California were generally inefficient, natural-gas plants with operating costs above the typical day-ahead price. Consequently, during the period January–August 2010 these plants ran at a loss every month. Beginning in September 2010, however, JPMVEC engaged in twelve new bidding strategies designed to optimize the outcomes it obtained in the auction. These strategies involved bidding so that the power plant actually lost money in producing the electricity, but more than made up for it in compensatory payments required to be paid to it from CAISO. In a presentation to JPMC, executives in the energy unit showed that for just two plants they operated between September and December in 2010, JPMVEC received $24 million in compensatory payments, had $14 million in market revenues, and had operating costs of $17.7 million. Thus, while operating at almost a $4 million loss, these units made a profit of $20 million!

What exactly did they do? Two strategies can illustrate the process. Strategy D involved exploiting what are known as ramp-up and ramp-down payments. Power plants take time to start up or shut down, and this physical feature is recognized in the CAISO rules. Strategy D took advantage of the fact that awards in the day-ahead market are made before CAISO knows the bids for the next-day market. This allowed JPMVEC to submit a low bid for the hour at the end of the day, and then submit much higher bids for the early hours of the next day, which had to be accepted because of ramp-down rules.

Figure 10 illustrates an example of this strategy. On Monday, JPMVEC would submit a bid of –$30.00 per MWh in the day-ahead market for the hour at the end of day on Tuesday (11 p.m.–12 a.m.). With such a low price, this bid was awarded a large quantity, at the market-clearing price. The next day (Tuesday), it submitted bids for the Wednesday hours between midnight and 2 a.m. These bids were for $999 per MWh. Because CAISO's system honors the minimum run time (in this example three

Figure 10

Strategy D

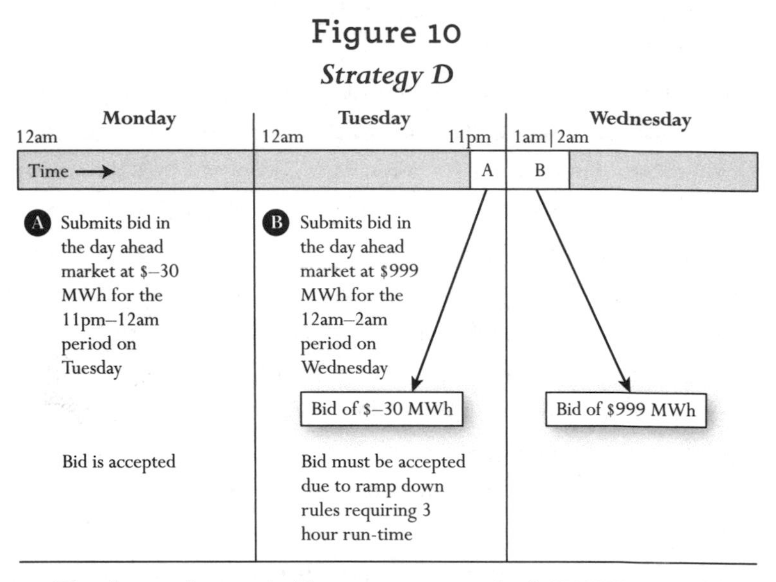

This figure shows a bidding strategy in which JPMVEC would bid in the day-ahead market to deliver energy for the last hour of next day (in this example, Tuesday) at a very low price. That bid is accepted on Monday. The next day, JPMVEC would bid in the day-ahead market to deliver energy for the first two hours on Wednesday. On the basis of the high price, the bid would have been rejected, but because minimum run time rules allowed ramp-down periods, the bid had to be accepted at the very high price.

hours), CAISO then had to give JPMVEC a ramp-down award for the next two hours at the unit bid price of $999. Prices in this time interval were typically around $12 per MWh, but with the ramp-down reward JPMVEC was paid $999 per MWh or $987 more than the market price![13]

Strategy A involved an even more elaborate (and profitable) bidding process designed to exploit "bid cost recovery" payments (or BCR). In this strategy, JPMVEC bid in the day-ahead market to provide a large amount of power at a price of –$30.00 per MWh.[14] As is required in the day-ahead market, it also turned in a Pmin value of, say, $10,000 for producing the plant's minimum production run of 100 MW (recall this amount was allowed to be twice its actual proxy costs). This would give JPMVEC an average bid of $2.50 per MWh (–$30 x 300 + 10,000) / 400 MWh = $2.50 per MWh). With such a low bid, it was awarded the full amount. The next day in the real-time market, it essentially "bought back" all but the Pmin amount by bidding in the real-time market at a price just above the market-clearing price. So, again for example, it would bid $35 per MWh in the real-time market. If the market-clearing price was $30 per MWh, then the ISO would instruct JPMVEC to produce only the minimum amount and "buy" back the extra amount. This left JPMVEC with producing only its Pmin level.

As FERC explained, this was an extremely profitable strategy because "JPMVEC was paid (as BCR) its full bid price [(e.g., $100/MWh)] for its Pmin energy, even with market prices averaging $30 to $35/MWh. In addition, JPMVEC received market revenues (i.e., the amount it was paid at market rates in the Day Ahead market less its Real Time buyback expense) for the same energy."[15] As an example of the profits, on September 22, 2010, HB4 (a power plant operated by JPMVEC) made $71,962 in market revenues and paid $106,567 in gas and operating costs, for a loss of $34,605 at market rates. But the unit received $159,987 in BCR payments from CAISO, for a daily profit of $125,382 despite losing money at market rates.

What is going on here? And why would anyone devise such a convoluted system in the first place? The answer to the first question is simply that JPMVEC exploited particular features of the accounting rules to allocate payments that were incorrectly set. Its ability to do so was not an accident; in July 2010, it hired John Bartholomew, a former intern at FERC, who in seeking a job at JPMVEC indicated on his résumé that he had found "a flaw in the market mechanism . . . causing CAISO to misallocate millions of dollars."[16] But even without his help, JPMVEC had been searching for ways to optimize its revenue given the auction designs it faced. Beginning in September 2010, its strategies focused on eliciting bid cost recovery payments, with the result that bid cost recovery payments paid by CAISO to producers soared from under $5 million per month in January 2010 to almost $25 million per month in January 2011.[17] An expert for CAISO testified, "The marked increase is due to a bidding practice that compels the ISO to commit a resource in the day-ahead market and then force the resource to be dispatched to the minimum load in the real-time [market]."[18]

The California ISO recognized that its auction rules were being taken advantage of and filed a request with FERC in March 2011 for expedited approval "to modify a market settlement rule to remedy the observed exploitation of the existing bid cost recovery tariff rules, causing an unexpected market outcome."[19] This action engendered even more strategies being developed by JPMorgan Chase. "According to FERC, JPMVEC continued creating new bidding schemes more than a year after it had been notified it was under investigation—even as CAISO . . . [was] re-writing the bidding rules to address the prior schemes. For example, after CAISO shut down one bidding scheme in April 2011, JPMorgan began two new schemes that led to another CAISO intervention in June 2011 to halt them as well."[20] In all, FERC Enforcement alleged that JPMVEC created twelve manipulative bidding strategies, ultimately costing CAISO $124 million.

Why was the auction design so complicated in the first place? The complexity of the underlying problem is surely the explanation. Auctions find prices for a wide variety of products, ranging from U.S. Treasury securities to Dutch flower bulbs, but even the simplest settings have to consider the incentive issues that face bidders. Here, the auction design involved two interconnected auctions determining prices and quantities hourly both in advance and in real time, compensatory side payments to elicit episodic participation by high-cost providers, and computerized algorithms generally programmed to consider each market and bid separately in allocating awards. The "optimal" strategies in terms of maximizing bidder's revenues in these auctions, however, were far more complex, and it is these strategies JPMVEC pursued.

What, then, to make of the ethical considerations here? One could argue that strategic behavior is a natural feature of auctions and that JPMC was only optimizing its position against a design that it and all other market participants faced. The strategies it pursued were within the particular limits of CAISO's bidding rules. Arbitraging the rules of the auctions as written did enrich JPMC, and in the process it revealed flaws in the auction design. This allowed CAISO to develop even better market designs. There are always winners and losers in auctions and in markets—being a winner is not a crime.

And yet . . . other considerations seem to be at play here. From a purely legal perspective, FERC argued that this was market manipulation, and as such was illegal. Following the Enron debacle, Congress passed the Energy Act of 2005, giving FERC "an intentionally broad proscription against all kinds of deception, manipulation, deceit and fraud." In turn, FERC's anti-manipulation rule prohibits "any act, practice, or course of business that . . . would operate as a fraud or deceit upon any entity; with the requisite scienter [i.e., intention]; in connection with . . . the sale of . . . electric energy."[21] FERC argued that JPMVEC's bidding strategy was designed not to make money based on market fundamentals but to "create artificial conditions" that would elicit payments from CAISO. This "defrauded the ISOs by obtaining payments for benefits (beyond the routine provision of energy) that JPMVEC did not deliver" and "interfered with and distorted the well-functioning markets in CAISO."[22] In short, JP Morgan Chase manipulated the market. In agreeing to settle this case, JPMC did not admit or deny the manipulation allegations, so as a legal matter whether it actually manipulated the market remains an open question.

From a broader ethical perspective, the role of motivation here seems crucial. JPMC developed strategies specifically to take advantage of the auction design, and not to actually meet the supply and demand needs of the market. By looking at the cash flows heuristically, recognizing that the compensatory cash flows were actually far more valuable than the cash flows from the sale of electricity, JPMC was able to arbitrage the electricity trading system. In doing so, however, it took advantage of a system designed to compensate good-faith bidders who were trying to offer power in a system striving to meet volatile demands. Producers who would have sold power were sidelined by a producer that wanted nothing more than to collect rents—and not actually sell power.

Much like our earlier example of stealing lemonade from a young child, taking advantage of the nonprofit ISO structure seems to me to be unethical. JPMC's actions did not improve outcomes in the market for anyone else, but instead distorted the functioning of the entire system. Its gains came at the expense of the ISOs, and the resulting increased costs affected the electricity prices and costs faced by every consumer. The motivations here ignored the larger ramifications of these actions on everyone else. Taking advantage of the market may or may not be illegal, but it is unethical. As discussed in chapter 5, the ethical limits of arbitrage are not simply what you can get away with.

Goldman Sachs and the Aluminum Market

In February 2010, Goldman Sachs bought an aluminum warehouse company called Metro International Trade Services. In November 2013, the Senate Permanent Committee on Investigations released a report, and held hearings, on Wall Street bank involvement with commodities, focusing, in part, on the seemingly bizarre behavior of the aluminum storage market. The committee echoed accusations first raised by the *New York Times* that Goldman orchestrated a "merry-go-round of metal," all "intended to exploit pricing regulations set up by an overseas commodity exchange."[23] The Senate report added,

> Goldman's ownership of Metro, Metro's rise to dominance in the U.S. LME [London Metals Exchange] aluminum storage business, and the long queues to remove metal from Metro have generated LME rule changes, Senate hearings, a *New York Times* expose, class action litigation, and ongoing allegations by industrial aluminum users that Metro's and Goldman's actions have increased aluminum prices and disrupted the aluminum market as a whole.[24]

Goldman Sachs, for its part, denied engaging in "improper merry-go-round operations," opined that the committee was evaluating the industry "through the wrong end of the telescope," and branded as "false" accusations that its actions caused aluminum to become more expensive to consumers.[25] Lost in this donnybrook is the basic question: was this behavior unethical?

The issues in this case involve a seemingly obscure corner of the aluminum market. Aluminum, which is used for everything from car parts to beer cans, trades both in physical commodity markets and in futures, options, and swaps markets. The physical market in aluminum is large, but so are the futures markets, with the bulk of aluminum futures trading on the London Metals Exchange (LME). Trading futures allows participants to hedge price changes by buying or selling aluminum contracts that expire at particular times in the future. Most futures contracts settle by offset; if you are "long" (you agree to buy), you enter a new "short" contract (you agree to sell), essentially canceling out the positions. You can, however, hold the futures contract to expiration, in which case the holders of short contracts must deliver aluminum to the holders of long contracts. In the 1983 movie *Trading Places*, that involved truckloads of oranges showing up at your house, but in the real world you actually just get a warehouse receipt.

An old saying in commodity markets is "If you can grade it, you can trade it," and that is a key factor in what is going on here. To be deliverable for futures trading, aluminum must be "warranted" by the LME, meaning that it certifies that the metal meets particular product quality specifications.[26] Owners of the aluminum pay for this warrant. Of course, the same aluminum may also trade in the spot market, in which case it need not be warranted. Warranted aluminum is held in LME-approved warehouses, which are operated by a variety of firms around the world. Owners of the metal pay the warehouse rent to store their aluminum. Goldman Sachs bought one of these aluminum storage firms, Metro International Trade Services (Metro).

According to the Senate report, in 2008 some 400,000 tons of aluminum were stored in U.S. LME warehouses, with Metro holding 52,000 tons, or about 12 percent. With the onset of the financial crisis, economic activity plummeted and, with it, demand for aluminum. This led to growth in aluminum stockpiles, so by February 2010 Metro alone was storing over 915,000 tons of aluminum. After its acquisition by Goldman, Metro followed an aggressive strategy of gaining U.S. market share in aluminum warehousing, reaching 70 percent in 2012, 78 percent in 2013, and 85 percent in 2014. By February 2013, Metro held 1.4 million tons of aluminum, nearly all of it warranted.[27]

To implement its strategy, Metro offered incentives to owners of aluminum to put their metal into Metro warehouses. These incentives, which according to Goldman were often in the form of "prebates" giving prepaid rent for several months, were also offered to some owners of metal currently in Metro warehouses.[28] It is these latter deals, combined with an obscure LME rule on moving aluminum out of LME warehouses, that are at the heart of the controversy here. In effect, Goldman would arbitrage the LME rules to create a "merry-go-round" of metal in Detroit (whether it was an *improper* merry-go-round remains to be seen).

To understand what Goldman did, we have be clear on the rules. The LME requires that an LME-approved warehouse must, if requested, move out a minimum of 1,500 tons of aluminum per day. Metro had twenty-seven warehouses storing aluminum in the Detroit area, but it operated a single queue for moving requests. So, despite its control of 80 percent or more of the stored aluminum in the U.S., Metro was required to move only 1,500 tons a day from across all of its warehouses.[29] An owner wishing to move its metal notifies the warehouse, the warehouse notifies the LME to cancel the warrant, and the owner joins the queue at the warehouse to move its metal. The metal could be re-warranted at a later date by paying the LME a fee.

With this as backdrop, consider a deal that Metro did with DB Energy Trading, a subsidiary of Deutsche Bank (DB) in September 2010. DB held 100,000 tons of warranted aluminum in Metro's Detroit warehouses, and it wanted a rent reduction. "According to Deutsche Bank, Metro proposed that Deutsche Bank cancel the warrants for the aluminum stored in the LME-approved warehouses, wait in the queue to load out the metal, transport the aluminum to other Metro warehouses, and after a period of less expensive or free rent, re-warrant the metal."[30] In addition, Metro offered to cap DB's rent while its metal was in the queue, and rebate to DB the moving cost of $42.95 per metric ton. So, by agreeing to this deal, DB essentially ended up with the same warranted aluminum, a lower rent, and a free ride for its aluminum around Metro's Detroit warehouses![31]

Why such a convoluted approach to a rent reduction? The key is the queue. Metro would ship only the minimum required 1,500 tons per day, so moving DB's 100,000 tons took sixty-five working days, during which time no one else's aluminum could be moved out of the twenty-seven warehouses. Of course, everyone waiting in the queue had to pay rent to Metro, meaning that the longer the queue, the more rent it received. And, by offering deals to select other aluminum owners in Metro's warehouses, Metro's queue could get longer and longer, with no way out for anyone wishing to move to another facility.

This strategy was astonishingly successful. As shown in Figure 11, the queue to move aluminum from a Metro warehouse increased from 40 days in March 2010 to 150 days in March 2011, to 300 days in March 2012, and to a mind-boggling 674 days in March 2014. For much of this time, Metro's forklifts and trucks simply moved metal from one Metro warehouse to another. Meanwhile, every client in the queue was stuck paying rent until its turn to load finally arrived. Not surprisingly, if you thought you ever wanted to get your metal out, your optimal strategy was to join the queue.[32] As noted by Bloomberg, in October 2013 the queue was 837,000 tons, equating to a wait of 445 business days (or 623 calendar days) at the then minimum load-out rates.[33] With 1.5 million tons of aluminum in the warehouses, this translated into more than half of the aluminum trying to get out.

Of course, one way to reduce the queue was to simply ship out more metal every day. But, as Goldman argued, "it is well understood by market participants that LME warehouses have

Source: U.S. Senate Permanent Subcommittee on Investigations, *Wall Street Bank Involvement with Physical Commodities*, p. 193.

an incentive to maximize inventory and rent and are likely to deliver metal at the minimum load out rate." And, the more rent it collected, the more inducements Metro could give to clients to move their metal to other Metro warehouses, causing the queue to grow longer still—in effect, creating a kind of "roach motel" in which aluminum could check in but not check out!

For its part, Goldman Sachs used a similar circular structure to assert that "Metro's incentive payments did not lengthen queues," which instead "were the result of metal owners' independent, financially-motivated decisions to remove metal."[34] That the owners were responding to the financial incentives Metro provided seems not to have figured in Goldman's calculus. What did figure in Goldman's reasoning was its reading of the explicit LME rules. The Senate report noted,

> Jacques Gabillon, Chairman of the Metro Board of Directors, as well as head of Goldman's Global Commodities Principal Investments group, told the Subcommittee . . . that, if metal associated with cancelled warrants was loaded back into the same warehouse from which it came, that would have violated an LME requirement that precludes warehouses from counting metal that is off warrant but "still on the Warehouse's premises" toward their load-out obligations. But the LME rules did not preclude a warehouse from loading out metal and then moving into a nearby warehouse belonging to the same company.[35]

Fortunately for Metro, moving metal across the parking lot to another Metro warehouse two hundred yards away was in Goldman's view perfectly fine.

What, then, to make of all this? Goldman entered into commercial warehouse agreements with its metal-owning clients.

The terms of these agreements were known to all parties. Offering incentives was not illegal, nor apparently was taking aluminum for rides around parking lots. Goldman adhered to the letter of the LME rules. Clients trapped in queues for over two years to get their metal out may have been understandably upset, but it does not appear that the behavior that led to this was actually illegal.[36] Perhaps, rather than deal with Goldman, these customers should have placed their metal in other warranted warehouses in the first place, none of which had substantial delays.

But is there more to the story? In particular, did the huge delays in getting metal out of Metro's warehouses affect the price of aluminum? Addressing this question is surprisingly complicated. Physical aluminum transacts at an "all in price," which is based on a variety of components. One of these is the "LME Official Price," which "is established through trading on the LME exchange and is generally recognized for aluminum as the "global reference for physical contracts."[37] Because metals are heavy, and users take delivery of them in different places, another component of the all-in price is a regional premium that reflects the costs of delivering aluminum in that locale. The premium to the LME price for aluminum sold in the United States is known as the "Midwest Premium." Figure 12 shows these aluminum prices.

Over the time period of interest, the all-in price of aluminum was generally falling. The Midwest Premium component of this price was steadily rising, however, from just over $100 in 2008 to more than $400 in 2014. This premium reflected "the price you pay to get aluminum today instead of when it comes out of a LME warehouse in two years."[38] Consequently, the gap between the LME and all-in prices grew increasingly large. Whether the all-in price was affected is debatable. Goldman and the LME argued that the rise in the Midwest Premium was offset by a fall in the LME price, so that consumers were no worse-off.[39] Others in the industry were less sure. What was less in question was that "the increasing difference between the all-in price and the LME futures price made hedging price risk through the LME market increasingly ineffective."[40] Because users of aluminum use hedging to handle risk, the machinations in the storage market affected the overall aluminum market.

Was any of this ethical behavior? In my view, it falls squarely into the "weasel zone." The delays in the aluminum market were not the result of normal commercial behavior, but stemmed from an explicit decision to exploit the storage queue rules. Whereas in our previous example JPMC took advantage of nonprofit ISOs,

Figure 12

Aluminum Prices, 2008–2014

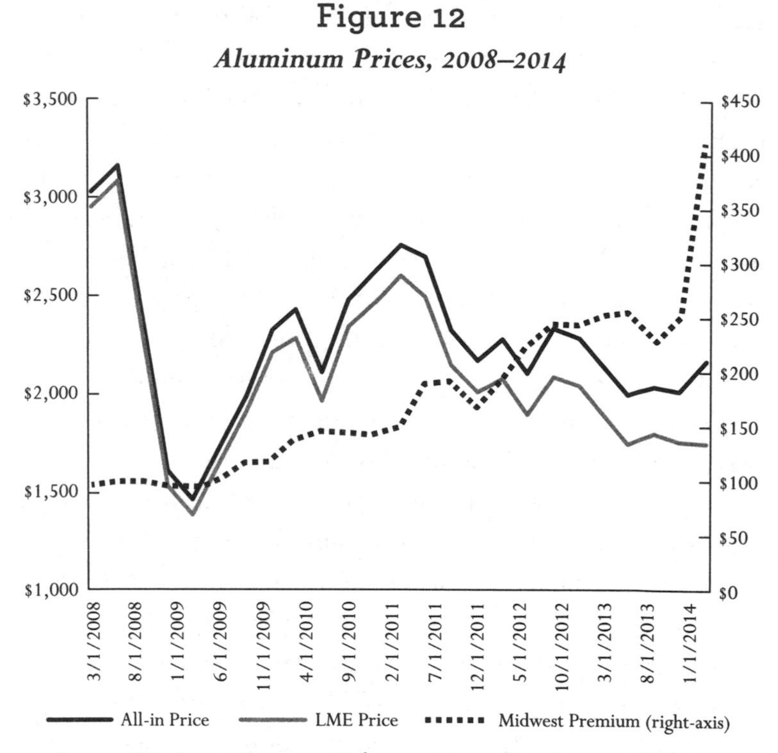

Source: U.S. Senate Permanent Subcommittee on Investigations, *Wall Street Bank Involvement with Physical Commodities*, p. 173.

here Goldman took advantage of corporate customers, most of whom were actually other financial firms. But the outcomes were similar—both banks extracted large rents from others by arbitraging rule structures set up to govern central markets. In doing so, they placed their own interests above that of everyone else, even to the point of interfering with the overall functioning of the market. Perhaps, as in the mouse experiment cited in chapter 1, there is something about markets that makes these ethical issues less salient, or maybe markets just make it easier to pull off bad behavior.

One might argue that Goldman was only following the rules, that it was the LME's fault for setting up such a stupid system in the first place. Yet, this argument misses the important fact that Goldman was one of the owners of the LME. In December 2012, the LME was sold to the Hong Kong Exchanges and Clearing Limited (HKEx), which in 2013 instituted new requirements linking the amount of aluminum to be loaded out in a month to the amount loaded into the warehouses. In November 2014, the LME also proposed changing its definition of "load out" to mean that it must be "delivered to a destination other than a warehouse of the same operator in the same location."[41] In December 2014, Goldman Sachs sold Metro International Trade Services.

CHAPTER 8

ARBITRAGING THE COMPLEXITY

> The complexity of things—the things within things—just seems to be endless.
>
> —ALICE MUNRO

ARBITRAGE OFTEN INVOLVES transactions within or across markets or venues. In earlier times, this could entail a simple strategy of buying in London and selling in New York. This still happens, but the proliferation of market venues combined with advances in technology dramatically changed the process. Now high-speed computers send orders along fiber optic, microwave, or laser linkages between New York, London, and potentially dozens of other markets in milliseconds. Algorithms trade where humans used to venture, allowing trading to be faster, cheaper, and exponentially more strategic. The advent of high-frequency markets has ushered in an age of complexity with a range of new ethical problems.

In this chapter, we address some of those ethical issues by

looking at arbitrage in the high-frequency world. As we will see, much of what goes on in high-frequency markets involves arbitrage, albeit now in a different guise. Arbitraging the complexity can improve the quality of markets, making traders better-off. But some of these arbitrage-based activities raise troubling ethical issues. Is setting up an algorithm to take advantage of another algorithm ethical? Are strategies that pose large risks to the entire market ever ethically acceptable? When does speed lead to unfair advantages over others in the market? As noted in the first chapter, the ethical issues here take gray to a whole new level of charcoal.

High-Frequency Trading and Statistical Arbitrage

High-frequency trading (HFT) is a seemingly precise name given to a wide range of imprecise activities.[1] At its core, HFT involves computer-driven trading done at very high speeds. The use of computers allows for strategies to be programmed into an algorithm, which is simply a self-contained step-by-step set of operations to be performed.[2] Some HFT activities are just faster versions of things long undertaken in markets, such as trading to exploit price differences between markets. Other activities are new, reflecting the dynamics that crop up in markets when billions of orders flow at speeds approaching the speed of light.

In such an environment, strategic behavior prevails, and algorithms are programmed to react not just to what has happened but to what is expected to happen. A prime example of this is statistical arbitrage. Whereas "classic" arbitrage involves exploiting actual price discrepancies, statistical arbitrage seeks to exploit expected price discrepancies. To understand this distinction, suppose we think about tracking the price behavior of every stock trading in a stock market. Using computers we could record the price of each trade and the time (to the millisecond) when it happened. We could then line up each of these price movements across all of the securities (you can see where computers come in) and observe how they correlate or vary with each other.

Suppose you see that when the price of stock A goes up, 99 percent of the time the price of stock B goes up right afterward (in statistical parlance, stock A leads and positively covaries with stock B). Then a simple strategy once you see stock A blip up is to sell stock A and buy stock B—sell high, buy low, so to speak.[3] Of course, stock B might not actually go up, but statistically this happens frequently enough that this arbitrage strategy will be expected to be profitable. Indeed, even a small edge in the probability that B will go up (50.9 percent instead of 99 percent, for example) will lead to expected profits over time.

Statistical arbitrage techniques underlie a variety of high-frequency strategies. High-frequency market making is a prime example. As we discussed in the preceding chapter, market makers provide liquidity in markets by being willing to buy and sell a security. Whereas traditional market making involved putting bid prices to buy and ask prices to sell the same security, here the HF market maker is putting in bids and asks in different securities. In the example above, a HF market maker will put in an offer to sell stock A and a bid to buy stock B. It—recall that an HF market maker is actually a computer program not a person—does so by putting limit orders into the electronic order book, where, if executed, the limit buy order trades at the bid price and the limit sell order trades at the ask price. If, as expected, stock B then goes up, the market maker has bought at the lower bid and can sell at a higher ask price. This provides liquidity to the counterparties of these trades, and profits to the market maker.

Statistical arbitrage is not risk-free. Although prices generally move in particular ways, they do not always do so. Pursuing strategies using millions (billions!) of orders, however, means that you have statistical power on your side. You also have another advantage: markets have rules about how they operate, and algorithms (i.e., computer programs) can also be thought of as setting out rules of what they will do. So HF strategies pay careful attention to these exchange rules and, as we will discuss shortly, to the rules defining other algorithms.

For example, an important feature of being able to implement the trading strategy above is to make sure that your order executes, and that depends upon where it is in the queue of orders in the limit-order book. Exchanges have priority rules regarding which orders execute first, and HF traders optimize against these rules to enhance their ability to be first in the queue. Being faster than everyone else, HF traders often submit, cancel, and resubmit orders to try to stay at the front of the queue. Of course, this causes all others to cancel and resubmit their order to try and stay ahead of the trader who just stepped in front of them. As a consequence, the vast majority of orders in U.S. equity exchanges (approximately 96 percent) are now canceled. As the chart shows, 40 percent or so of orders (quotes) that are fully or partially canceled do so within 500 milliseconds.[4]

Despite these cancellations, the order book (or more precisely, the number and placement of the orders in the book) is an important input into many HF strategies. This is because the book may indicate (at least over the very short time frames of interest to high-frequency traders) future price movements. If there are many orders queued up to buy and few to sell, for example, it may indicate an increased demand for the stock (or at least incipient liquidity pressure on the sell side). HF strategies may then try to capitalize on these predicted effects by stepping in front of the queue (i.e., posting a slightly higher price to buy) or by putting in orders to provide liquidity (i.e., posting orders to sell) at attractive spreads.

Other market variables may also signal future price movements. Sequences of buy (sell) trades may signal that a large order is being chopped up by an algorithm and that more orders will be coming, pushing prices up (down). Similarly, higher volume may indicate greater interest in the stock, as could trades of large sizes, or trades in the same stock occurring across different markets, or trade patterns across the day, or movements in

Figure 13

Quote Lifetime: Corporate Stocks

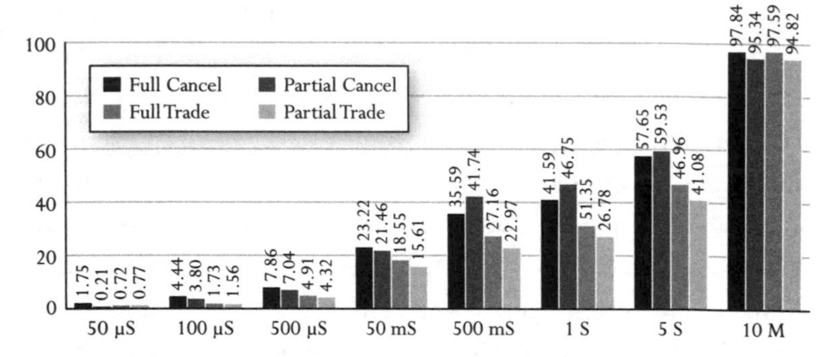

This figure shows how long orders last before they are canceled or executed. Time is measured in microseconds (μS, or millionth of seconds), milliseconds (mS, or thousandths of seconds), seconds (S), and minutes (M). The chart measures the cumulative lifetime of orders; so, for example, 97.84 percent of all fully canceled orders are canceled within 10 minutes or less, 35.49 percent of all fully canceled orders are canceled within ½ second or less, and 1.75 percent of all fully canceled orders are canceled within 50 microseconds. This chart is taken from SEC Market Analysis, "Equity Market Speed Relative to Order Placement," March 19, 2014.

related futures or options markets—all of these trade data can be informative in regard to trading interest in the stock and so portend future movements in the market. HF strategies incorporate these variables into algorithms designed to exploit these potential profit opportunities over very short intervals of time. Much like classic arbitrage, if successful these statistical arbitrage strategies provide profits without the HF firm's having to commit large amounts of capital—in effect, a very fast version of "something for nothing"!

Some have accused HF traders of "front running," in that their strategies often "step in front" of others' trades.[5] Front running traditionally occurs when a broker (who knows his customer's order) trades ahead of the customer—for example, buying the stock right before he executes his customer's buy order. Since buying pressure will generally raise the price, the broker will capitalize by selling after the price increase. Of course, the broker's trade may have also caused prices to increase, meaning that he has disadvantaged his own customer. This behavior is both illegal and clearly unethical.

What HF traders do is different. They are not brokers and thus do not know customer orders. They do try to infer what those orders might be by watching for patterns in order flows. There is nothing illegal (or in my view unethical) in doing this, although it does mean that other traders now have to trade more carefully. Where this gets complicated is when HF traders can always step in front of orders owing to their superior speed or access to trading information, an issue we discuss later in the chapter. First, however, we consider HFT strategies that seem designed to cross the lines of ethical behavior.

Training Your Algorithms— when HF traders Go "Bad"

When HF traders provide liquidity, other traders are able to transact at what are now historically low spreads. When HF traders arbitrage price differences across markets, prices in markets become more "efficient," the term in finance used to describe prices that reflect all available information. Certainly, exchanges love the volume generated by HF traders, allowing them to operate deep, active, and (for the exchange) profitable markets.

But the high-frequency age also provides opportunities for unethical behavior, much of it directed to fooling the machines that now manage trading for both high-frequency and non-high-frequency players. These machines use algorithms to send in orders to exchanges and venues. A large institutional trader, for instance, a pension fund like CALPERS (the California Public Employees Retirement System), might want a large trade in a security executed at the lowest transactions cost. To do so, its broker uses a VWAP (volume-weighted average price) algorithm to chop the order into smaller pieces that are then executed across the day. An index trader like Vanguard might want to trade a large amount at the close of the trading day, and so its broker uses a "market on close" algorithm that tries to optimize its orders to execute at a reasonable end-of-day price. Algorithms can also help traders find liquidity in fragmented markets by using "smart routers" to send orders to disparate markets or to alternative trading venues like crossing networks. And, unfortunately, algorithms can be written to take advantage of these algorithms, essentially by using the power of computers to take advantage of other computers (and the customers whose orders are behind those trades).

Consider, for example, a "quote dangling" algorithm. Quote

dangling is a strategy that tries to "trick" another algorithm into bidding against itself.[6] Suppose that a broker algorithm is trying to execute a buy order for its client and puts a limit order into the book at the bid price. Currently, there are no sellers at that price, so the order will wait at the top of the queue until a seller appears. A quote dangling algorithm now sends (and instantaneously cancels) many limit orders to buy at prices just above the resting limit. These orders can trick the broker's algorithm into thinking there is more buying interest in the stock and therefore move its limit price higher, in effect bidding against itself. The dangler then sends and immediately cancels more orders at prices just above this new limit price, trying to keep this process going and induce further bid price increases. At some point, the dangler algorithm will hit the bid price by sending in a market sell order, profiting by selling at the now inflated price.

A related and very similar deceptive practice is layering. Here is how the *Wall Street Journal* described this strategy:

> A trader might buy a small number of shares at $10 and place an order to sell them for $10.10 on an alternative trading venue, such as a dark pool. He also places a series of large orders to buy this same stock on an exchange for higher prices—$10.20, $10.30, $10.40—"layering" on orders that create an impression of strong demand. When this apparent demand prompts other participants to raise their "buy" orders to $10.10, the trader's "sell" order is executed and he instantly cancels his large buy orders, pocketing a 10-cent-a-share profit.[7]

Why do these strategies work? In part, because they take advantage of predictable behaviors in standard algorithms set up to execute trades for other traders. They also work because this all happens so fast (often within milliseconds) that it is impossible for humans to observe and react, leaving it up to the computer program to decide what to do. Yet another reason is that it can be very difficult for regulators to sort out the manipulative behavior from other, perfectly legitimate trading strategies that also involve order placements and cancellations. Perhaps the most basic reason is that, as in the mouse experiments discussed in chapter 1, the anonymity of the market, combined with the abstraction of writing lines of code, obscures the reality that it is not just another computer program being exploited.

The Dodd-Frank Wall Street Reform and Consumer Protection Act of 2010 specifically forbids "spoofing," which it defined "as bidding or offering with the intent to cancel the bid or offer before execution."[8] While this definition certainly applies to a variety of seemingly manipulative practices, it can also describe other strategies that are not per se illegal, such as "pinging," or sending a small order between the spread to see whether there is hidden liquidity in the book of orders and canceling if there is not. Despite this lack of clarity, the regulators have been much more active in pursuing "spoofing" cases, particularly when the behavior seems egregious.

A case in point is Panther Energy Trading and its principal Michael Coscia. In July 2013, the firm settled charges (without admitting or denying guilt) with the Commodity Futures and Trading Commission (CFTC) that it "made money by employing a computer algorithm that was designed to illegally place and quickly cancel bids and offers in exchange traded futures contracts." The particular strategy it pursued was a form of layering in which the firm would enter large orders in one direction (for example, sells) as well as smaller orders in the other direction (buys) at prices off the current quotes. The large orders were intended to suggest momentum in the stock price, causing other traders to think that prices would be moving higher or lower. These price movements would trigger the profitable execution of the small orders, Panther would cancel the large orders, and then repeat the scheme in the opposite direction. Indeed, of the 460,000 large orders placed by Coscia, only 371 were completely filled.[9]

The CFTC fined Panther $2.8 million and imposed on Coscia a one-year ban from the market. Britain's Financial Conduct Authority levied an approximately $900,000 fine for similar trading strategies used by Panther on the ICE Futures Exchange. In October 2015, the U.S. Department of Justice argued its first criminal case for "spoofing," charging Michael Coscia with six counts of commodities fraud and six counts of spoofing.[10] Central to the government's case was the argument that Coscia's algorithms were designed to mislead other market participants. The defense's claims that the Dodd-Frank prohibitions were too vague and did not actually specify a standard for what is and is not spoofing apparently were not convincing to either the judge or the jury. After only one hour of deliberation, the jury found the defendant guilty of all charges.[11]

Other cases feature similar behavior. In September 2012, the SEC and the Financial Industry Regulatory Authority (FINRA) fined Hold Brothers On-Line Investment Services almost $8 million "to settle allegations that they allowed deceptive trades from overseas outfits to pass through their trading systems without proper risk controls." Hold Brothers allegedly signed up traders in China and other foreign countries to trade through its trading systems. FINRA noted that it discovered "hundreds of instances where the foreign day traders used spoofing and layering activities to induce the trading algorithms of unwitting market participants to provide the trades with favorable execution pricing."[12]

An even more troubling case is that of Swift Trading, a Toronto-based firm that in 2008 had almost four thousand traders operating in far-flung countries, including China, Nicaragua, and Romania. According to the *Wall Street Journal*, Swift's volume was so large it was a "top-10 trader on the Nasdaq Stock Market by volume." FINRA charged Swift in 2012 with failing to establish a supervisory environment to "prevent a pattern of manipulative trading activity." In 2011 the British Financial Services Authority imposed on Swift "one of its largest fines ever (8 million pounds) for engaging in market abuse."[13] These cases, as well as a regulatory case filed against Swift by the Ontario Securities Commission in 2012, focused on layering strategies.

In an interesting variation on this theme, the high-frequency firm HTG Capital in March 2015 filed a civil suit against an unnamed "Doe Defendant," alleging "egregious manipulation" in the Treasury futures contracts traded on the Chicago Board of Trade. The lawsuit contends that "the Doe Defendant engaged in an illegal form of market manipulation known as 'spoofing'" and that "this practice enabled the Doe Defendant to manipulate the market to their benefit and to the detriment of HTG and other market participants."[14] It remains to be seen whether the civil courts will be an effective venue in which to address such market trading issues.

Not all cases involve spoofing, however. In October 2014, the SEC charged Athena Capital Research with trading manipulation at the close, in what the SEC noted was "the first high frequency trading manipulation case." The SEC found that Athena developed a specialized algorithm named Gravy to enter orders "in the final two seconds of almost every trading day during a six-month period to manipulate the closing prices of thousands of NASDAQ-listed stocks."[15] This allowed Athena to overwhelm the available liquidity at the close and artificially push the closing price in Athena's favor. The SEC's head of enforcement stated, "Traders can certainly use complex algorithms and take advantage of cutting-edge technology, but what happened here was fraud." Athena Capital Research settled with the SEC without admitting or denying the findings.

In May 2013, the CFTC adopted a new Rule 375 to clarify what constitutes prohibited disruptive trading practices. The new rule focuses on spoofing behavior as well as "quote stuffing"—a trading practice in which an algorithm submits and cancels massive numbers of orders with the aim of overloading an exchange's quotation system, thereby delaying other traders' executions. The rule also requires that such messages be entered in "good faith for legitimate purposes."[16] It remains to be seen how effective this rule will be in curtailing such behavior.

Unethical behavior in markets is not new, and market manipulation has long been illegal. But manipulation has always been difficult to prove, in part because legally you have to prove that the intent was to affect prices artificially, and not just to make trading profits.[17] The speed and stealth made possible by computerized trading in the high-frequency age make it even more difficult to meet this legal standard. The legal issues will be front and center in a high-profile criminal case filed on April 21, 2015, against Navinder Singh Sarao; the case charges wire fraud, market manipulation, and spoofing in trading futures in the period June 2009 through April 2014. Particular interest has focused on Sarao's trading on May 10, 2010, the day of the "flash crash."[18] Sarao allegedly manipulated the e-mini S&P 500 futures market by using a "layering" strategy of placing large sell orders into the book at prices three, four, five, or more ticks above the market price.

The criminal complaint explained, "The trader seeks to mislead and deceive investors . . . by creating a false appearance of market depth, with the intent to create artificial price movements. The trader could then exploit this layering activity by simultaneously executing other, real trades that the trader does intend to have executed, in an attempt to profit from the artificial price movement that the trader had created."[19] In effect, knowing that computer strategies often use the imbalance of orders in the book as a signal of future price movements, this trader allegedly placed bogus sell orders into the book with the sole purpose of putting downward pressure on the futures price—once it fell, he would buy at the artificially lower price before prices rebounded to their nonmanipulated level.

An interesting legal wrinkle in this case is that it actually predates the implementation of Dodd-Frank, so the case will focus on more standard manipulation and fraud issues. The issue of intent may be easier to prove, however, because the complaint alleges that Sarao used a specially written algorithm that included "a cancel-if-close function, so that an order is cancelled if the market gets close."[20] As in the case involving Michael Coscia, it may be hard to convince a jury that a legitimate trading strategy features orders that can never be executed.

Although the legal issues may be contentious, the ethical case against these practices is far easier to make. Trading designed only to take advantage of others, to disrupt the market for personal gain, is unethical. It is not trading in "good faith" (or, as Aristotle put it, "dealing justly"); it sets the individual's gain above the "collective happiness of society [or the market] as a whole"; it is not doing "the right thing for the right reason." It jeopardizes the entire market and the efficient pricing it provides. It is simply wrong, no matter which ethical framework you consult.

When Does It Become "Unfair"? Data, Speed, and High-Frequency Trading

More interesting (and perplexing) ethical issues attach to other features of the high-frequency world. High-frequency trading relies on ultrafast computers (often with custom-built chips capable of processing information in nanoseconds), dedicated microwave or laser transmission lines (that send orders in milliseconds), and colocation of its computer servers within the exchange to give its traders a speed edge over other traders. High-frequency traders also rely on proprietary data feeds from exchanges to give them trade information a split second before it is seen by others on the consolidated tape. At what point do these HFT advantages become "unfair"?

That some traders are faster than others is not new, and often this speed advantage has come from technology. David Leinweber, in his entertaining book *Nerds on Wall Street: Math, Machines, and Wired Markets*, provides a fascinating account of the evolution of trading and technology.[21] Baron Rothschild was said to have used carrier pigeons to receive news of Napoleon's defeat at Waterloo and so trade before everyone else. The introduction of the telegraph in the 1850s set off a land rush to buy buildings next to the NYSE so that runners could take incoming orders there as quickly as possible.[22] The stock ticker, invented in 1867 and later perfected by Thomas Edison, gave market watchers by the 1920s new information before other, less technologically savvy traders received it. The list of technological innovations designed to make some traders faster than others goes on and on—right up to the current building of a new laser link capable of sending orders a few nanoseconds faster between Carteret, New Jersey, where Nasdaq's data center resides, and Mahwah, New Jersey, the site of the NYSE's data center.[23]

Of course, it is not just traders who are interested in being at the head of the line. The passengers on the *Titanic* discovered that being in third class was not as good as being in first class when it came to seats in lifeboats. Frequent travelers are promised the right to board the airplane first, making it harder for other travelers to secure overhead storage space. Even Universal Studios offers Express Pass Access to travelers staying at the park's hotels, allowing guests to jump to the head of the queue for popular rides simply by showing their room key.[24] In each case, paying more gets you priority access over those paying lesser amounts.

This also describes the situation in stock trading. HFT firms pay technology firms like Anova for using its laser link, or for any of the other enhanced linkages that speed their orders via faster channels to the market. Exchanges charge substantial fees for users wanting to colocate their computers, with varying fees depending upon whether you want fast, faster, or fastest access. Exchanges also charge for proprietary data feeds, giving purchasers not only faster access to data but also more enhanced data, such as limit-order information that will never be available otherwise. Is this really any different from paying extra to avoid the lines at Universal Studios? Or is it basically unfair because it has the potential to create a two-tiered market (one for them and one for us) in which the market for us works worse?

The exchanges would argue that speedier access is not unfair, because they are happy to provide it to anyone who wants to pay for it. For most traders, such access is irrelevant because their trading needs are not so time sensitive that a few milliseconds actually matter. For other traders, particularly those engaged in intermarket arbitrage, that is not the case. If you are trying to arbitrage between and across disparate markets, lags in access introduce execution risk, making the extra cost of enhanced access a necessary investment. Because traders do not all start out the same, it is not surprising that some want to pay for upgrades and others do not.

The same logic can also apply to market data. Exchanges charge for proprietary data feeds, giving purchasers more and faster access to data than is available to other traders. As David Leinweber points out, "you are what you eat, and algos eat market data."[25] This is particularly true about market data on the state of the limit-order book. But the production of that data is not free; the vast number of cancellations and resubmissions requires exchanges to invest heavily in infrastructure to manage this data avalanche. Selling data to traders who need and use such data (as opposed to simply sharing the costs equally across all market participants) is akin to charging a user fee—an outcome most economists would argue is a fairer pricing scheme.

And yet . . . something about all of this is disquieting. Is the market that confronts various traders the same market, or is it fundamentally different for some traders? Despite equal access, is the resulting market unfair? For that matter, what does it mean to be unfair?

Earlier we discussed how fairness plays a key role in the Ethical Culture movement, but of course it is also central to the other ethical frameworks we considered. The notion of fairness traces back to Aristotle, who stated that "equals should be treated equally and unequals unequally."[26] As Manuel Valasquez, Claire Andre, Thomas Shanks, and Michael Meyer explain, "In its contemporary form, this principle is sometimes expressed as follows: 'Individuals should be treated the same, unless they differ in ways that are relevant to the situation in which they are involved.'"[27] One implementation of this principle is that something is unfair if it shows favoritism or discrimination. Velasquez, Andre, Shanks, and Meyer explain further, "Favoritism gives benefits to some people without a justifiable reason for singling them out; discrimination imposes burdens on people who are no different from those on whom burdens are not imposed. Both favoritism and discrimination are unjust and wrong."[28]

These concepts provide an interesting lens through which to view ethical issues in high-frequency markets. In January 2015, the SEC fined BATS Global Markets the largest amount ever levied against a stock exchange ($14 million) over how two exchanges operated by its subsidiary Direct Edge handled customer orders. The specific issue involved complex "price sliding" orders that differed in execution and priority treatment from more-standard orders. The SEC's director of enforcement commented, "These exchanges did not properly describe in their rules how their order types were functioning. They also gave information about order types only to some members, including certain high-frequency trading firms that provided input about how the orders would operate."[29] This suggests that having properly described orders available for traders to use (or not use) is not the problem. Only telling some traders and not others about these order types is favoritism, and it is clearly unfair.

Favoritism and discrimination also arise in other high-frequency settings, particularly in contexts relating to information. The *Wall Street Journal* reported in June 2013 that a widely watched consumer sentiment statistic, the University of Michigan's consumer-confidence report, was being released to certain traders minutes before it was released on the university's website and to the news wires at 10 a.m.[30] These privileged recipients were clients of the Thomson Reuters Corporation. In return for paying varying fees to that company, the clients obtained the report five minutes early or, if they subscribed to the "ultra-low latency distribution platform," received it in machine-readable format even earlier, at 9:54:58 a.m. For getting such distribution rights, Thomson Reuters paid the university $1 million per year.

The university initially defended the practice, arguing, "Without a source of revenue, the project would cease to exist and the benefits would disappear."[31] Among those who were not convinced was Attorney General Eric Schneiderman of New York, who launched an investigation into the practice. An early critic of the deal was Bloomberg, which, according to the *Wall Street Journal*, had protested awarding the contract to Thomson Reuters in 2007. In a communication to the university, it complained, "While we were offering money to help the University create a system that is fair to everyone, they are paying you to guarantee an unfair one!"[32] In October 2014, the university ended its arrangement with Thomson Reuters, moving to a new distribution arrangement with Bloomberg that ended early access. In doing so, the university noted, "This agreement . . . supports our strong commitment to open access to research data."[33]

The issues here illustrate the blurred lines between information and news in the high-frequency age.[34] Both private information and public information (news) can affect stock prices, and a broad range of regulations and practices (such as company earnings announcements via press releases or required filings given first to the SEC) are designed to turn private information into public information. It was widely believed that the University of Michigan data was news—information that was created by a publicly funded entity and distributed publicly, not privately. Had Michigan placed a disclaimer on its website ("This announcement was actually seen five minutes ago by high-frequency traders *who* have long since traded on it"), the furor surrounding this situation might not have arisen.[35] But such was not the case. The notion of favoritism, of a public entity being compensated to allow others to take advantage of the unknowing, made what the University of Michigan did seem unfair—and unethical.[36]

Yet, in this high-frequency world even the most scrupulous can run afoul of the problems introduced by the speed. A recent academic paper by Jonathan Rogers, Douglas Skinner, and Sarah Zechman entitled "Run EDGAR Run: SEC Dissemination in a High-Frequency World" found that filings to the SEC's EDGAR system were being seen in advance of their public dissemination by a select group by paying customers.[37] EDGAR (Electronic Data Gathering, Analysis and Retrieval System) is the main portal for all SEC corporate filings, and it is via this portal that the public accesses this information. The SEC does not actually operate EDGAR but instead hires a contractor to handle the technology and run the system. This contractor, in turn, offers subscribers for $1,500 a month a direct feed to these filings. SEC rules require the contractor to send the documents to the SEC website and to the subscribers at the same time, but the research found that the SEC website could take "anywhere from 10 seconds to more than a minute [longer] to post the documents" after it received them via the direct feed.[38] This discrepancy resulted in trading volume and price surges in companies' stock during the interval, consistent with traders' acting on (and profiting from) their earlier access to information. In the wake of Congress's condemning this as "[violating] the basic principles of fairness that underpin our markets," the SEC has promised that it is "conducting a thorough assessment of the dissemination process."[39]

There is a certain irony here, given that in 2012 the SEC fined the NYSE $5 million for "compliance failures that gave certain customers an improper head start on trading information."[40] The issue concerned NYSE data being sent to proprietary feed customers before it was sent to the consolidated tape. Robert Khuzami, director of the Division of Enforcement, stated, "Improper early access to market data, even measured in milliseconds, can in today's markets be a real and substantial advantage that disproportionately disadvantages retail and long-term investors." The director of the Division of Trading and Markets added, "Our rules require exchanges to distribute information on quotes and trades to the consolidated data processors on terms that are 'fair and reasonable' and 'not unreasonably discriminatory.'"[41]

These cases highlight two issues particularly relevant to the concept of fairness (and ethics) in markets. One is that making the data available is not a seamless process. Even if the data are sent out at the same time (for example, from the NYSE or from the SEC's contractor), it may not reach all end users at the same time. Building the consolidated tape, for instance, takes time, as does posting the documents on the EDGAR system. Perfect coordination is unlikely to be attainable, and so neither is perfect fairness. Perhaps the best that can be hoped for is equal access to the various data streams, although this seems a less than satisfactory solution.

A second issue has to do with the notion of "not unreasonably discriminatory." Defining "reasonable discrimination" is challenging, in part because it relates back to our initial concept that fairness requires that individuals be treated the same "unless they differ in ways that are relevant to the situation in which they are involved." A recent example from Disneyland illustrates the distinction here. Disney had a policy of allowing those with disabilities to avoid standing in line and get express access to rides. However, the system was discontinued in part because of "the phenomenon of disabled 'tour guides' who charge money, sometimes hundreds of dollars, to accompany able-bodied guests and allow them to avoid long lines."[42] Discriminating in favor of the disabled seems both reasonable and fair; profiting by exploiting the system is unreasonable and unfair, both on the part of the disabled tour guides and their able-bodied clients. As we have discussed before, putting your needs above those of others is unethical.

In security market settings, sorting out the fair from the unfair is not an easy task. Because traders in markets are different, it seems unlikely that the same solution will always apply. Some traders need speed to implement their strategies; others do not. Some need to trade using complex algorithms; others can send in simple market and limit orders. Allowing the markets that face traders to differ can be fair provided those differences do not put the needs of some traders above those of everyone else. Finding the ethical boundaries here is unlikely to be straightforward, leading to markets that may at least appear to be "more fair" for some than for others.

CHAPTER 9

ARBITRAGING THE RULES REVISITED

As we have seen throughout this book, arbitrage can be used for a wide variety of purposes, some good and some not. When arbitrage activities are helpful, they remove market inefficiencies and make market participants better-off. When arbitrage activities are used to deceive or to exploit other market participants, they cross the line into unethical behavior. But discerning that line, particularly when arbitrage activities are used to get around rules and regulations, is not always easy. These ethical issues become even more challenging when the incentives of the parties involved are considered. While it is easy to decry the incentives of the bankers structuring the deals, the incentives of the client are also important to consider. Is something unethical if it is exactly what a client wanted (until it turns out badly)?

In this chapter, we revisit the topic of arbitraging the rules by looking at these incentive issues in connection with two applications. One involves the issue raised at the outset of the book—were Goldman Sachs' actions in helping Greece remove debt from its balance sheet ethical? Before we address this question, however, it is helpful to look at another intriguing episode in Europe—the problem of "toxic loans." Both cases use the techniques of modern finance to arbitrage accounting rules in Europe. Both ended badly, but were they unethical?

Toxic Loans in France

In 2011, a French government committee issued a report following its investigation of toxic loans in French municipal finance. The report found that over two thousand towns and municipalities in France had entered structured loans with a value of 30 billion euros, and that unrealized losses on these loans were estimated to be 10 billion or more euros. Equally alarming, many of these loans had decades remaining until maturity, with interest rates linked to derivatives tied to exchange rates (particularly the Swiss franc) or to other exotic features like the slope of the interest rate yield curve. Though many of these loans were originated by the troubled Belgian bank Dexia, others were made by Deutsche Bank, Royal Bank of Scotland (RBS), and other mainstream European lenders.[1] Is this yet another example of banks taking advantage of unsuspecting borrowers, or is there more to the story?

To understand how this crisis developed, we first need to be clear on what defines a toxic loan. As discussed earlier, a structured loan is a bank loan with an embedded option. These loans can be straightforward (as in our chapter 3 example), but they can also be exceedingly complex. The toxic loans in question were generally long-term (twenty, even thirty years was not uncommon), featured an initial period in which interest rates were fixed at a very low rate, and had subsequent interest rates tied to a formula based on a given financial index. The low initial rates arose from option premiums paid to the borrowers, who wrote long-term options on the financial indices. Typically, these options were initially "out of the money," meaning that at current index levels the options would entail no payment. Over time, however, these index levels could move, making the options valuable to the holder (the lender) and expensive to the option writer (the borrower).

Loans with embedded foreign exchange options were particularly popular because the inherent volatility in exchange rates meant that option premiums were high, causing initial interest rates to be very low. Indeed, an interesting study of toxic loans by Christophe Pérignon and Boris Vallée cites the example of a zero percent coupon loan entered into by the city of Saint-Etienne. This loan had a maturity of thirty-two years, with interest payments in the first nine years fixed at zero percent, and in the remaining years staying the same provided the euro–Swiss franc exchange rate remained below the euro–U.S. dollar exchange rate.[2] If, instead, the exchange rate moved higher, then the interest rate increased to reflect the payoffs due on the now in-the-money option. As with option contracts in general, there are no limits on how high these interest rates (aka option payoffs) can go.

Why would municipalities enter such exotic contracts? Several points are relevant here. One is that French municipalities are not permitted to borrow to finance operating budgets; loans are instead intended to finance only new investments. The interest on debt does appear on financial statements, but just in the year it is incurred. A second contributing factor is the absence of organized municipal debt markets. Whereas U.S. municipal borrowing takes place via bonds, European municipal borrowers rely primarily on bank loans. Financial institutions like Dexia developed specialized expertise in creating structured products for these municipal borrowers. A third motivating factor lies in the opaque accounting treatment of derivatives; accounting standards in many European countries do not require the disclosure of derivative transactions.[3] Thus, with interest rates pegged abnormally low for the early years, and no need to even report the derivative portion of the loan, these structured loans appeared to be a great deal—at least for accounting purposes.

The financial crises brought these illusions to a halt. Many borrowers found interest rates soaring from their initial levels. The village of Sassenage saw rates rise from 3.5 percent in 2009 to more than 15 percent in 2011.[4] The city of Saint-Etienne faced rates of 24 percent in 2010 because its borrowings were indexed to the British pound–Swiss franc exchange rate.[5] The Swiss National Bank's decision on January 15, 2015, to allow the Swiss franc to appreciate has only compounded these problems. Bruz, a small town in Normandy, will see the interest rate rise to 28 percent on its Swiss franc–indexed loan.[6]

Perhaps not surprisingly, some municipalities have balked at paying the now higher interest rates, arguing that the banks arranging the deals did not explain sufficiently the risk inherent in their structure. The courts, however, have not been particularly receptive to these arguments, although the government of France did set up a special agency to deal with the fallout of the Dexia bankruptcy.[7] Certainly, if banking institutions misrepresented the risks of these loans, or took advantage of borrowers' inexperience to sell them loans that benefited only the lender, then this behavior was unethical, if not also illegal.

But there are other explanations worth considering. These loans were entered into by elected officials. The accounting treatment of derivatives certainly gave towns and villages an incentive to book the early monetary gains and ignore the back-loaded risks. Borrowing money (with abnormally low initial interest payments) could allow for municipal spending that would otherwise be unavailable. While such spending may well have been in the municipalities' best interests, it is even more likely to have been in the politicians' best interests. Agency problems between managers and owners can often result in suboptimal actions within firms; the same agency problems can also arise between politicians and the electorate.

It is never possible to discover exactly what officials thought were the risks, but it is possible to investigate whether the borrowing behavior of municipalities is consistent with these political incentives. This is the focus of the research study by Christophe Pérignon and Boris Vallée, who examined borrowing data from almost three hundred French local governments as well as data on structured loans made by Dexia. They provide intriguing evidence that political incentives played a role in these borrowing arrangements. For example, they found that "incumbent politicians running in politically contested areas are more inclined to use toxic loans."[8] They also found that "elected representatives from financially distressed local governments are significantly more likely to turn to this type of loan" and that "structured loan transactions are more frequent shortly before elections than after them." Certainly, the ability to spend now and pay later—often much, much later is tempting to a politician, particularly if you do not expect to be the one in office years later who will have to pay.

Could it also be the case that these politicians simply did not understand the contracts? Possibly, but again Pérignon and Vallée present evidence against this lack of financial sophistication explanation. They find that "politicians whose profession requires higher education are more inclined to use toxic loans than politicians from a less educated background, and politicians from large cities are more likely to use toxic loans than the ones from small towns." Perhaps it is true that a little knowledge is a dangerous thing.

What, then. to make of the ethical issues here? Certainly, one can feel sorry for towns and villages now encumbered with large debts, and one can question the judgment of the politicians who entered into these loans. If elected officials entered into those loans solely to promote their own careers at the expense of the citizens' welfare, then their actions were clearly unethical. But was it ethically wrong for the banks to make these loans? Here I think the issues require more thought. Structured loans are so familiar a feature of European municipal finance that one study determined that more than 72 percent of the largest local governments use such financing structures.[9] Most of these loans involve basic structures tied to interest rates and not to the exotic indices that resulted in toxic loans. In some venues, such as the United States, suitability restrictions on municipal borrowing would have precluded banks from offering these exotic lending arrangements.[10] But France had no such rules, so towns and villages were free to take on (and banks free to offer) these derivative-based loans.

Should the banks have refused to make the loans because the borrowers should have shown better sense than to take them out? I think that is a tricky argument to make. Exploiting the rules on derivative accounting or the lack of suitability rules was widespread in Europe, in part because municipalities wanted to take on more risk in the hopes of lowering their borrowing cost (or at least pushing it off to the future). For many municipalities, these loans did not work out well, but elected officials entered freely into these contracts, choosing to take the risk on behalf of their constituents. Banks, having greater expertise in these areas, should have advised against doing so when appropriate, but it is not clear to me that they have the right to impose their views over those of elected officials. While it may have shown poor judgment to take out these loans, it does not seem to me to have been unethical to make them.

Greece, Goldman Sachs, and All That Debt

We began this book with the controversy over the way Goldman Sachs structured complex financial transactions to allow its client Greece to "remove" debt from its balance sheet. Critics charged that Goldman helped Greece "cheat" its way into the eurozone by arbitraging accounting rules to mislead the market about the true state of Greek indebtedness. Goldman insisted that it did nothing wrong. Having investigated the tools of modern finance, examined the role of arbitrage in markets, and explored the ethical dimensions of a variety of cases, we can now turn to the question we posed in that first chapter—was Goldman's conduct ethical?

The transactions in question occurred in late 2000 and early 2001, when Greece was struggling to meet the Maastricht rules limiting government debt to less than 60 percent of GDP and yearly deficits to no more than 3 percent of GDP.[11] Greece, like many European countries, borrowed heavily in global markets, accessing the vast liquidity available in U.S. dollar- and yen-denominated debt. European rules required unhedged currency–denominated debt to be translated into euros using year-end currency rates, and the revaluation caused by the strengthening dollar and yen in the fall of 2000 increased Greece's official debt. How, then, to lower its official indebtedness to the deficit ratio required by the Maastricht rules?

Goldman Sachs proposed a series of financial transactions to achieve this goal. The exact details of the transactions remain opaque because of confidentiality agreements, but the key to this strategy was to use cross-currency swaps in which Greece would give Goldman dollars or yen and Goldman would give Greece euros.[12] As we discussed earlier, swaps are generally zero-sum contracts in which the parties swap payment streams. This currency swap differed from a standard transaction in that Goldman structured the swap by using "an historical implied euro exchange rate" rather than the prevailing rate. This weaker exchange enabled Greece to exchange yen or dollars for more euros, essentially giving Greece a loan of approximately 2.8 billion euros.

To repay the loan, Goldman and Greece entered into a long-dated interest rate swap in which Goldman paid a fixed rate and Greece paid a floating rate whose value was determined by a preset formula. According to Bloomberg News, "the [interest rate swap] deal had a notional value of more than 15 billion euros, more than the amount of the loan itself." The swap also featured a "'teaser rate,' or a three-year grace period, after which Greece would have 15 years to repay Goldman Sachs."[13] These swaps are essentially variants of the structured loans taken out by municipalities that we discussed earlier in this chapter.

Two features of these transactions are particularly important. One is that, as Goldman stated, they "reduced Greece's foreign denominated debt in Euro terms by €2.367 b[illio]n."[14] Second, these transactions were essentially invisible to the market because European rules in force at that time treated currency swaps (and derivatives in general) as nonreportable events. Consequently, the "loan" from Goldman to Greece was not reported to Eurostat, the European Union's statistics agency in charge of calculating debt metrics and the like, and so was not reflected in Greece's metrics. As Goldman also noted, "The Greek government has stated (and we agree) that these transactions were consistent with the Eurostat principles governing their use and application at the time."[15]

What seems clear is that these transactions accomplished deficit reduction not by changing the fundamental borrowing or lending of the Greek government but rather by exploiting the accounting treatment of derivative transactions. Moreover, the existence of strategies to arbitrage these rules appears to have been well known to market officials. As the *New York Times* observed, "These kinds of deals have been controversial within government circles for years. As far back as 2000, European finance ministers fiercely debated whether derivative deals used for creative accounting should be disclosed. The answer was no." Indeed, it would take until 2008 for Eurostat to change the accounting rules governing these transactions.[16]

By using the tools of modern finance, Goldman Sachs clearly made Greece better-off in 2001. In doing so, it also made itself better-off, earning a fee reported to be as high as $600 million. But what of the ethical issues here? Is it scandalous, as Angela Merkel suggested, to help countries "fake the statistics"? Or is Goldman correct that it did nothing wrong in helping its client Greece meet its financial needs?

As we have seen throughout this book, detecting these ethical lines can be challenging. Earlier we argued that Lehman Brothers Repo 105 crossed the line because its sole purpose was to deceive, thereby putting the managers' interests above those of the shareholders, the market, and everyone else. Certainly, in some ways, this transaction is similar in that the extent of Greece's indebtedness was hidden from the market. But unlike in the Lehman case, the techniques used here actually were known and approved by the regulators. Indeed, JPMorgan introduced this technique in 1996 when it created a currency swap deal for its client Italy that featured a similar (hidden) embedded loan structure (and a similar purpose). While the "everyone else is doing it" defense is generally not a compelling ethical argument, it does raise the question of who was actually deceived by practices that were being used more generally in the market. It does not seem unfair if everyone else can, and in some cases did, do the same thing.

Was it unethical for Goldman to arbitrage what in retrospect were suboptimal rules on the accounting treatment of derivatives? I think it is hard to make this argument. Given the rules of the market, Goldman solved a problem on behalf of its client. In doing so, it broke no laws and acted in its client's best interest. Much as in the case of toxic loans, market outcomes might have been better if regulations had precluded such activities, but it is always easier to see in hindsight what was not apparent at the time. Indeed, from another vantage point, you could even argue that Goldman actually helped the fledgling eurozone system by enabling new members to join. While I suspect Goldman Sachs may share this view, this positive spin is a bit too much for me (and probably for most people).

That it was Goldman Sachs, and not JPMorgan, that came under fire for this technique illustrates an interesting feature of ethical perceptions. Behavioral research has established that people's perceptions of what is ethical are influenced by the outcome of events. For example, Francesca Gino, Don Moore, and Max Bazerman describe an experiment in which individuals are asked to judge the ethicality of decisions made in drug testing, product manufacturing, and auditing contexts.[17] Other individuals are asked to do the same, but they are told in advance of doing so the outcomes of these decisions. Results clearly show that respondents rate decisions with bad outcomes as being far more unethical than those with good outcomes. Such outcome-dependent ethics may be consistent with behavioral biases, but it is not consistent with any ethical frameworks we have discussed.

In this case, recall that the Goldman-Greece transaction was little known when it occurred in 2001 and that it came to light only in 2010. By that point, the European sovereign debt crisis was well underway, and Greece was playing a starring role. Greece's subsequent problems seemed to attract far greater censure to Goldman's actions than to the similar, but earlier, actions that JPMorgan took on behalf of its client Italy. It is hard to see how what is ethical for Italy's bankers is unethical for Greece's bankers.

There is, of course, the interesting issue of whether Greece or Italy (or more precisely, their politicians) acted ethically, as opposed to just their bankers. One could argue that the countries were more culpable, but then again the actions they took were allowed by the European regulatory framework. The Greek government was freely elected and presumably made decisions that it thought were in the best interest of its citizens—a position Aristotle would surely have supported.

Out of the Fog . . .

CHAPTER 10

RECOGNIZING THE BOUNDARIES

WHAT IS THE role of ethics in modern finance? We began this book by questioning the role of finance in society and asking whether the tools and techniques of modern finance were being used to exploit others, to take advantage of the complexity of modern markets to behave unethically. Arbitrage plays a starring role in modern finance, and when used productively arbitrage techniques can be tremendously beneficial, providing something positive for society at little or no cost. But these techniques can be (and unfortunately sometimes are) abused—and when they are abused, finance serves to enrich the few at the expense of the many. In my view, when this happens the failure is not with finance but with the ethics (or lack thereof) of the practitioners.

Is it enough to simply say that these problems have more to do with criminality rather than with ethics? That an arbitrage-based activity is acceptable provided it does not break some explicit legal rules? I think even the most die-hard legal advocates know that this is not true. Many things in society are not strictly illegal but are widely understood to be unacceptable. A recent XKCD cartoon makes this point with respect to stealing baskets of taco chips from Mexican restaurants.[1] As a diner scooping all the chips into a bag to take home observes, "*They're the ones giving the chips away. If they don't see the arbitrage potential, sucks for them!*" Stealing chips from Mexican restaurants places you firmly in the "weasel zone" and so, too, do some of the activities in the case studies we have examined. Perhaps, as the cartoon opines, society functions only when you do not take these people out to dinner—or let them play a role in the financial markets.

Even granting the vital role that ethics plays in markets and society, it is not always a simple matter to recognize ethical boundaries when they arise in market settings, particularly when ethical issues appear in new or unique circumstances. Can we always spot ethical dilemmas when they crop up? Probably not, but research in behavioral ethics suggests that you are more likely to do so if you are aware of the inherent biases that affect ethical decision-making. In this chapter, I briefly describe some of these biases, with the goal of suggesting how to recognize when the use of financial techniques can cross ethical boundaries.

A second issue concerns implementation. If, in fact, the difficulty in behaving ethically lies with the "barrel maker" and not just with the bad apples, then issues in the broader environment cannot be ignored. Certainly, the environment within financial firms has to be considered, looking, as it were, to the "barrels" for insights into why some firms seem to avoid ethical problems while other firms move from one scandal to the next. These issues go under the general rubric of culture, and they speak to the difficult problem of how to create an environment in which individuals are willing and able to put ethical decision-making into practice. This issue has been of concern to bank regulators who wonder how banking can be made responsible for its actions—or at least cognizant of its failings in this regard.

A deeper problem is the general environment surrounding ethical issues in finance, particularly as it affects the people who work, or will work, in the markets and corporate world. One could view business schools as the "barrel makers," as the settings in which the role and central importance of ethics is imparted to future business leaders. In this context, there is clearly work to be done. Finance has largely been agnostic about ethical issues, with finance professors leaving them to be discussed instead by ethics professors. Despite the popularity of ethics courses in business education, there is ample evidence that this "silo" approach (ethics at 10:10 a.m. on Mondays and Wednesday, Finance at 1:20 p.m. on Tuesdays and Thursdays, etc.) is not succeeding. Finance educators and scholars have to explicitly recognize the role of ethics in finance, making clear the integral role that it plays in making finance a positive, and not a negative, force in society. I end this chapter by examining these important issues.

Behavioral Ethics

Behavioral research has identified a wide range of perception issues that arise in connection with ethical decision-making.[2] For example, as David Messick and Max Bazerman establish, people generally think they are more honest and trustworthy than other people. People are more critical of others' ethics than of their own, and they are more suspicious of others' motivations for doing good acts (Epley and Caruso). People are also far more likely to believe that other people are more self-interested and motivated by money than they are (Ratner and Miller). These findings, and others like them, have led to a field of study called behavioral ethics. Behavioral ethics draws on research in evolutionary and social psychology, neuroscience, and economics to try to understand why people act in ways that seem inconsistent with their espoused beliefs. Whereas philosophical-based theories of ethical behavior start with determining the principles of right and wrong and then behaving accordingly, behavioral ethics is more intuitive than rational, with individuals believing that their actions are ethical given the circumstances they face.

Fundamental to this field is the process of moral disengagement. In his influential work *Social Foundations of Thought and Action*, Albert Bandura argued that individuals have personal standards of moral behavior that serve a self-regulatory role in guiding their behavior. This self-regulatory function, however, can be deactivated in selective circumstances, a process he termed moral disengagement.[3] As James Detert, Linda Treviño, and Vicki Sweitzer explain, "[T]hrough moral disengagement, individuals are freed from self-sanctions and the accompanying guilt that would ensue when behavior violates internal standards, and they are more likely to make unethical decisions."[4] Thus, moral disengagement occurs when you know something is wrong in principle but you do not recognize it as applying to specific circumstances.

Bandura identified a variety of mechanisms that can lead to this result, including moral justification, displacement and/or diffusion of responsibility, and attribution of blame. Examples of these mechanisms at work include companies justifying the employing of workers overseas in dangerous sweatshop conditions because without this job the workers would be employed in even more dangerous low-paying conditions. Or, employees who view what they do as simply following directives from their boss, and so feel no culpability for any resultant unethical act (a phenomenon also pointed out by Stanley Milgram in his famous shock experiments in 1974).[5] Ubiquity also seems to play a role, and Warren Buffett's famous dictum "The five most dangerous words in business are 'Everyone else is doing it'" captures the problem that the diffusion of responsibility can lead to moral disengagement. Indeed, individuals can even blame customers for bad outcomes that result from unethical actions ("they should have read the fine print more carefully" or "they should not have borrowed that money in the first place"), absolving themselves of any guilt in the matter.

What leads people to ignore ethical problems that seem patently obvious to others? One big factor is self-interest. Max Bazerman and Ann Tenbrunsel explain, "It is well known that people see what they want to see and easily miss contradictory information when it is in their interest to remain ignorant." Such "motivated cognition" and "confirmation-seeking bias" are at the heart of the eighteenth-century philosopher David Hume's statement that "no amount of observations of white swans can allow the inference that all swans are white, but the observation of a single black swan is sufficient to refute that possibility."[6] Unfortunately, all too often people focus only on the white swans that they want to see and not on the black swans that are inconvenient to admit.

This tendency can lead to a problem called "motivated blindness," in which people overlook unethical behavior by others when it is in their self-interest to do so.[7] Bazerman and Tenbrunsel give the example of professional baseball, where league officials seemingly ignored the rapidly increasing size and strength of home run hitters, perhaps because attendance was higher when more baseballs were being hit out of the park. That steroid use was more responsible for these home runs than enhanced weight training or better coaching seemed much more obvious to people outside of baseball than to insiders.

Motivated blindness can play a role whenever a conflict of interest arises for decision-makers. Countrywide's decision to sell mortgages to other investors that it did not want to hold on its balance sheet may have reflected such a motivated blindness, as may have Bank of America's decision to package up loans that it knew were not meeting the standards it had portrayed to the investors and ratings agencies. As we discussed earlier, this behavior is exacerbated by compensation schemes that reward employees for meeting particular tasks (offloading mortgages), rather than for meeting more general goals such as selling quality products to all customers. For decision-makers, the key to avoiding this problem is to be highly cognizant of conflicts of interest and to solicit objective (nonconflicted) views of potential ethical issues in such circumstances. It is also crucial to design compensation schemes that motivate and reward positive behaviors and that do not incentivize individuals to focus narrowly on a specific task.

Behavioral ethics pinpoints a wide range of other biases that can cause unethical behavior. Omission bias, for example, reflects the widely found tendency for people to judge harmful actions as being far worse than equal harm caused by inaction.[8] Rather topically, this omission bias is often mentioned with regard to the decision of some parents not to have their children vaccinated.[9] If failure to vaccinate can lead to more expected harm to society than the remote chance of complications from the vaccination, is not omission a more serious ethical failure than commission? While leaving this question to the ethicists, we note that similar issues arise in financial markets. As we discussed in the *SEC v. Goldman Sachs* case, not telling the buyers of the synthetic CDOs about the role Jon Paulson played in selecting the reference portfolio may have been viewed as less unethical (or perhaps as not unethical at all) than explicitly lying about his involvement. Yet, if the harm caused is the same in each case, is there really any ethical difference? Reducing the impact of omission bias in decision-making requires careful review of all aspects of a transaction—both what you do and what you fail to do matter.

"Indirect blindness" is another behavioral bias that can undermine ethical behavior. Indirect blindness refers to the decrease in perceived severity of harm, moral wrong, or moral accountability resulting from the delegation of acts to an agent or other intermediary. As Paharia, Kassam, Green, and Bazerman cogently observe, "Mobsters have hit men. CEO's have vice presidents, lawyers, and accountants."[10] When actions are undertaken by others, the ethical consequences can seem less immediate. An example here is when drug companies sell a product to another company that in turn dramatically raises the price (as happened in February 2015 when Valeant Pharmaceuticals International bought the rights to two heart drugs and immediately raised their prices by 525 percent and 212 percent).[11] Experiments by Paharia et al. using a generic drug company setting found that subjects rated increases as being far more unethical if implemented by the original company than if implemented by the new company, even when the seller knew the new owner intended to raise the prices to much higher levels.

Indirect blindness may play a particularly important role in financial markets because of the extensive usage of subsidiaries in the corporate structure of financial firms. As of December 2013, Citicorp, for example, had 1,997 subsidiaries in which it held a 50 percent or greater interest, Wells Fargo had 1,570, JPMorgan Chase had 1,246, and Goldman Sachs had 356 (the "winner" among financial institutions was BNP Paribas with 2,460 subsidiaries).[12] Returning to our earlier analysis of the aluminum market, was it easier for Goldman Sachs (the parent) to ignore potentially unethical behavior in Metro International Trade Services because it was not happening directly within Goldman

Sachs but rather in a subsidiary company? Similarly, was Merrill Lynch less in tune with the mortgage origination failings because these originations were done by third-party agents? There is no way to know, but behavioral research suggests that delegating actions to others is a pitfall in ethical decision-making because it can lead to delegating the responsibility for ethical oversight as well.

Solutions for this problem can be challenging. Companies often set up subsidiaries to allow for independence of operations, but this independence in turn can thwart efforts to enforce uniform standards across an organization. Enforcing accountability for actions across and within the firm is fundamental to avoiding diffusion of responsibility. Even hit men have to answer to someone, and so should executives who delegate decision-making to others.

Another intriguing bias identified in experimental research is the tendency to make ethical determinations on the basis of the outcome of an event. A medical researcher who fudges the results of clinical trials of a drug, for example, is deemed less unethical if the drug ends up being successful than a similar researcher who fudges results and the drug causes someone to die.[13] Both researchers cheated, but the good outcome somehow seems to overshadow the initial corrupt action. This translates in a corporate setting into rewarding outcomes instead of decision-making. While Napolean may have preferred his generals to be lucky rather than good, it is not clear that instilling ethical behavior in a corporation works on the same principle.

Can this same effect occur in reverse, with events with bad outcomes viewed as being more likely to emerge from unethical actions? It seems obvious that it does, and Goldman Sachs' dealings with Greece seem to me to fall into this category. Had Greece gone on to become a successful member state of the eurozone, issues connected with its complex borrowing in 2001 might well have been ignored in the same way that Italy's earlier very similar borrowings were. But as Greece played a large role in the subsequent European sovereign debt crisis, finger pointing emerged and, with it, suspicions that what Goldman and Greece did was somehow unethical (if Italy's economic problems continue, a similar revisionist view of its lending behavior may occur in the future). Ethical decision-making is not, and should not be, outcome dependent.

The influence of outcomes can also manifest itself in a bias called the "identifiable victim effect." Here the issue is that the harm from unethical behavior seems less salient the farther away, or less identifiable, the victim is. Research has shown that people care more about identifiable victims than about "statistical victims," setting the stage for actions to appear less unethical if the victim is not immediately identifiable. Indeed, if the harm is far enough away, actions may seem to have no ethical consequences at all. This problem is likely to be acute in modern financial markets, where transactions occur in impersonal securities markets, and trading strategies are developed by writing code rather than by interacting with real live buyers and sellers.

Certainly, the problems we have discussed with mortgage-backed securities, spoofing strategies, and bidding in electricity markets all feature this impersonality. But so do many other settings, and that underscores why recognizing this bias is particularly important. The engineers at Ford, for example, knew that people would suffer as a consequence of the design flaw in the car. These statistical victims, however, did not seem to merit much weight in the decision process, or perhaps more ominously they did, but the cost-benefit analysis did not attach as much weight to the costs as to the profits. Addressing this bias requires keeping the focus on the broader consequences of decisions, on the fact that somewhere there is someone on the other side of these deals. Markets may be impersonal, but they are not depopulated—actions that hurt the "market" really do affect other people.

Finally, another behavioral bias relevant for finance decision-makers is the "slippery slope" problem, or the tendency to overlook ethical problems if they develop slowly over time. Recent experimental work by Welsh, Ordóñez, Snyder, and Christian used an intriguing three-period study to see how cheating changed over time when payoffs to doing so were gradually increasing or were abruptly changed.[14] They found that participants were twice as likely to lie in the third round of an experiment if the payoffs to doing so increased gradually from the first period rather than changed abruptly in the last period. Similarly, research by Max Bazerman and his coauthors entitled "Why Good Accountants Do Bad Audits" determined that experimental participants playing the role of auditors were more likely to miss exaggerated results if they had approved smaller (and also incorrect) incremental results.[15]

This incremental bias speaks to the problem of recognizing when a process has morphed into something different from what it was at the start. The JPMorgan Chase Ventures Energy case discussed earlier may reflect this difficulty. The initial problem facing the unit was how to restore profitability to its energy trading. Having found that changing its bidding strategy could lead to more profitable outcomes, the unit then went on to introduce more drastic bidding strategies, ultimately becoming engaged in what the market regulators would call manipulation. Indeed, this process grew so involved that JPVEC appeared to be in almost a cat-and-mouse struggle in which the regulators would shut down one alleged manipulative strategy only to have the energy trading unit develop a new one. Once the chase is on, it may be hard to remember why you are doing what you're doing—and why this may not be a good idea.

The list of behavioral biases actually goes on and on, but the ones highlighted here—motivated blindness, omission bias, indirect blindness, outcome bias, incremental bias—seem to play key roles in explaining why some unethical behaviors persist in banks and financial markets. Perhaps recognizing that such biases characterize decision-making in general can help reduce the prevalence of poor ethical decision-making. Or, at the very least, it can highlight why it is necessary to address ethical issues at the organization level and not just trust that individuals will always naturally recognize and "do the right thing."

The Role of Culture

Groucho Marx once opined, "The secret of life is honesty and fair dealing. If you can fake that, you've got it made." Unfortunately, in the case of financial institutions, their ability to achieve even that seems to have faltered. William Dudley, president of the Federal Reserve Bank of New York, argues that "there is evidence of deep seated cultural and ethical failures at many large financial institutions."[16] Mark Carney, head of the Bank of England, points to "a malaise in corners of finance that must be remedied."[17] Christine Lagarde, managing director of the International Monetary Fund, deplores "the behavior that continues to deplete the treasury of trust and could again destabilize the global economy."[18] Even the Archbishop of Canterbury is chiming in, noting that "the culture of banking became contaminated in commercial banks."[19]

What exactly is this "culture" that has gone awry? Dudley asserts, "Culture relates to implicit norms that guide behavior in the absence of regulations or compliance rules. . . . It is how people react not only to black and white, but to all of the shades of grey."[20] William Cohan suggests that "it is the behavior that occurs when other people aren't watching."[21] I think culture reflects what we have discussed throughout this book; it is the ethical framework that drives people to recognize that just because you can does not mean you should. Whether financiers originally had this recognition or, more cynically, simply convinced others that they did, the problem now is that no one is buying it. And with $138 billion in fines in the United States alone (and counting), the problem has gotten out of hand.

Academic research calls for a broader view of culture, suggesting that both ethical culture and ethical climate contribute to the firm's overall ethical infrastructure. Ethical infrastructure is affected by formal systems (such as codes of ethics, corporate policies, and so on) as well as by informal systems (behavioral norms, company traditions, and the like) that transmit values throughout the corporation. Linda Treviño contends that when the signals from these two sources are conflicting, the ethical culture of the company is viewed as weaker.[22] As discussed by Sean Martin and coauthors, "empirical work generally supports the expected negative relationship between perceptions of the organization's ethical culture and unethical behavior."[23]

That dissonance between formal and informal systems can undermine an ethical culture may have been a point not appreciated at Goldman Sachs. In recent litigation, investors accused Goldman of making misleading disclosures regarding how it sought to avoid conflicts of interest. The disclosures in question included these statements from its code of ethics and other corporate documents: "Our reputation is one of our most important assets," "Integrity and honesty are at the heart of our business," and "We have extensive controls . . . to address conflicts of interest."

In arguing why this case should be dismissed, Goldman offered a rather surprising defense. As the *New York Times* reported, "it asserted that [the statements] were only opinions and, at worst, constituted statements investors would not take seriously—essentially, the salesman's assertion that no one believes a product really is the 'best,' 'fastest' or 'revolutionary.'" Goldman also argued that "the statements were not 'material' because reasonable investors would not consider these important." The judge in the case, apparently not finding this argument convincing, noted, "If Goldman's claim of 'honesty' and 'integrity' are simply puffery, the world of finance may be in more trouble that we recognize."[24] Perhaps for Goldman the informal dimensions of culture will have to do double duty given the firm's views of the formal dimension.

How do you change a culture that is not working? There are a variety of ideas on this, but the exact template for doing so remains unclear. It is tempting to think that culture can be changed by decree–that regulators can simply require better behavior through new rules and enforcement mechanisms. As Martin Wheatley of the UK's Financial Conduct Authority has explained, "The traditional regulatory mechanism for dealing with cultural weakness has always been to enhance the rules. To close loopholes in the law as and when they appear. To require more disclosure or compliance with specific processes." But he continues, "The problem with this approach is two-fold. First: it is static. So it is closing the barn door after horses have bolted. Second—and perhaps counterintuitively—we know it can encourage the behavior it seeks to stamp out."[25] Christine Lagarde echoes this concern, noting that "people who want to skirt the rules will always find creative ways of doing so. So we also need to turn attention to the culture of financial institutions, and to the individual behavior that lies beneath."[26]

William Dudley argues that this cultural change has to come "from the top": "Senior leaders need to hold up a mirror to their own behavior and critically examine behavioral norms at their firm." Fundamental to this "must be a respect for the law" and a willingness to self-report violations and infractions. He also points to the need for changing the incentives of bankers, particularly through changes in compensation practices.[27] These areas of focus seem particularly appropriate in view of results discussed by Andrew Ross Sorkin in his article "On Wall Street, a Culture of Greed Won't Let Go."[28] He reports that in a 2013 survey of financial industry insiders, 26 percent "believed the compensation plans or bonus structures in place at their companies incentivize employees to compromise ethical standards or violate the law." In response to another question, "15 percent doubted that their leadership, upon learning of a top performer's crime, would report it to the authorities." The 2015 survey of that same question is not encouraging: now 17 percent believe it unlikely that company leaders would report misconduct to authorities.[29]

This start-at-the-top sentiment is shared by the newly created British Banking Standards Review Council, which noted, "It is for them [the leaders of the institutions] to define the values and purpose of the banks which they lead, to appoint and promote people who are aligned with its values, to decide which types of business they are happy to accept and which to turn away, and to do everything in their power to make sure that the tone set at the top reaches all the way down through these often very large organizations."[30]

But how exactly does this "tone at the top" inform the far reaches of an organization? James O'Toole and Warren Bennis argue that it happens because "the leaders' job is to create systems and norms that lead to a culture of candor."[31] A culture of candor results from an environment of transparency in which the norms of the organization are clear and discussed by all. Such an environment can limit the power of managers who view access to information, and the discussion that can ensue, as threatening to their status and control. Transparency, in turn, can break down barriers such as "group think" that can lead otherwise ethical individuals to be unwilling to speak up against what appears to be the prevailing view.

This lack of candor can be a problem both in financial firms and in their regulators. The 2013 General Accounting Office report investigating why the SEC did not detect Bernie Madoff's Ponzi scheme (although it had been given almost a complete road map of the operation by a whistle-blower) concluded that the SEC was hierarchical and risk averse.[32] The report cited one person's complaint that "managers have been afraid to close cases or make decisions because senior officers want to minimize the chances that they would be criticized later."[33] Certainly, this reflects the problem of operating effectively when the underlying culture is not conducive to open dialogue and discussion.

Yet, even getting it right within the firm may not be enough to address the ethical issues in the financial sector. As we saw in chapter 5, Mark Carney points to a need for individuals and firms to have a sense of responsibility for the financial system. He argues for an "inclusive capitalism" in which individuals not only take responsibility "for themselves and their families" but also "have a sense of their responsibilities for the broader system."[34] To do this, he asserts, bankers and financiers must build "a sense of vocation."

An intriguing approach to achieving this goal is a new initiative of the Dutch Banking Association.[35] Starting in April 2015, all ninety thousand bankers in the Netherlands have been required to take the following oath:[36]

I swear within the boundaries of the position that I hold in the banking sector

- *that I will perform my duties with integrity and care;*
- *that I will carefully balance all the interests involved in the enterprise, namely those of customers, shareholders, employees and the society in which the bank operates;*
- *that in this balancing, I will put the interests of the customer first;*
- *that I will behave in accordance with the laws, regulations and codes of conduct that apply to me;*
- *that I will keep the secrets entrusted to me;*
- *that I will make no misuse of my banking knowledge;*
- *that I will be open and transparent, and am aware of my responsibility to society;*
- *that I will endeavor to maintain and promote confidence in the banking system.*

So truly help me God.

Bankers have a year in which to take the oath, or find new employment.

Will this change banking culture in the Netherlands? It remains to be seen, but it is having an effect on at least one Dutch bank. Bloomberg reports that the initial public offering of the reconstituted ABN Amro bank (once the largest bank in the Netherlands that merged into other banks in 2007 and was then revived under Dutch government ownership during the financial crisis) was postponed by the Finance Ministry following reports that the senior management behaved in a manner inconsistent with the oath.[37] In particular, the bank's six top executives received 100,000 euro pay raises (on top of base salaries of around 700,000 euros), causing parliament to convene hearings and a commentator to note that the bankers were "thinking harder about earning than serving." These raises have now been given back, and the IPO has taken place. Perhaps the bankers are now thinking more about serving—or maybe just about leaving for more lucrative pursuits.

The Dutch efforts speak to a desire to change the culture more broadly, to instill a greater ethical awareness and sense of responsibility into those making decisions in firms and markets. While starting with those already in managerial positions seems sensible, it seems even more fruitful to instill such awareness into people before they take those positions. This requires looking to the "barrel makers"—to the universities and business schools—to play an important role in training graduates to have such skills. And it particularly requires finance professors and researchers to consider the part they play in highlighting, or obfuscating, the role of ethics in finance.

I am not sanguine that universities will take up this challenge. Whereas a hundred years ago the goal of training men and women to be "of high moral character" played a prominent role in at least the rhetoric at universities, today it is more likely found only in some dusty mission statement. This argument has been made cogently by William Deresiewicz in his book *Excellent Sheep: The Miseducation of the American Elite and the Way to a Meaningful Life*, in which he criticizes what he terms the commercial ethos of modern universities. While some have objected to the stark characterizations in that book, the notion that universities no longer view the instilling of a moral code as part of their mission is not really in question.[38] Perhaps like the swimming requirement for graduation now in place at a mere handful of universities (including mine), the notion that ethics is part of an educated person's portfolio has become outdated.

Business schools, however, have responded differently, making ethics courses now a mainstay in virtually every business curriculum. I suspect these courses do help raise the profile of ethical issues, highlighting the perplexing ethical dilemmas, for example, attaching to Nike's factories in Asia or to the challenges of operating businesses ethically in countries rife with corruption. And many students are clearly influenced by them, as exemplified by the movement in 2009 to establish an "MBA oath" to act with integrity both within and outside of their employer.[39] But actual take-up of the oath has been limited, and one could argue that those motivated to do so may be more ethically minded to begin with—a selection bias that could still leave certain industries (finance comes to mind) little changed.

I think finance has to change its view toward what it is we are teaching. Using finance tools to build new, socially useful financial products makes both buyers and sellers better-off. Rather than simply "taking advantage" of arbitrage opportunities, we should be seeking to use financial techniques to improve markets, to reduce the costs of transacting, to create new products that remove financial complexity. Teaching students to view finance in this way requires abandoning the agnostic view of finance as a set of tools that can be applied to any and all situations indiscriminately. Luigi Zingales, in his recent presidential address to the American Finance Association—entitled "Does Finance Benefit Society?"—raises exactly this point: "Is being agnostic subtly teaching students the most amoral behavior, without us taking any responsibility?"[40]

I think it is doing that, and the solution is to provide more context so that students can appreciate not only how to use these tools but also when and why to do so. In this endeavor finance research can play an important role by highlighting when financial tools and practices help (or hurt) firms, markets, or individuals. Examples of such research are the William Christie and Paul Schultz papers documenting price-fixing on the Nasdaq market in the 1990s; David Yermack's work on the timing of stock option awards in firms; and recent work by Luigi Guiso, Paolo Sapienza, and Luigi Zingales investigating, from a finance perspective, the value of corporate culture and in particular perceptions of integrity for a firm's performance.[41]

Will changing how we teach and do research to focus more on using finance to create positive value for society change the ethical climate? I am not sure, but I do believe that to affect the role that ethics plays you have to return to individuals and to the choices that they make. Certainly incentives can influence these choices, giving importance to things like compensation schemes, corporate penalties for noncompliance, and the severity and probability of legal sanctions. Still, these factors all play to the notion that self-interest alone determines ethical choices, which may be true for some but is surely not the case for all. As we discussed in chapter 4, there is a wide range of ethical frameworks that help people avoid falling into the "weasel zone."

How can the behavior of individuals not so sure of those other convictions be made more sensitive to ethical considerations? Here the advice of Aristotle may prove useful—"we become just by doing just acts, temperate by doing temperate acts, brave by doing brave acts."[42] Perhaps the key to becoming ethical is to do more ethical acts. For a start, pass on stealing those chips in the restaurant—and deciding on other, more important issues may become easier.

CHAPTER 11

THE ETHICAL LIMITS OF ARBITRAGE

I BEGAN THIS BOOK as a quest to understand the intersection of arbitrage and ethics in modern finance. The tools of modern finance can make markets (and people) better-off, but the same tools and techniques used inappropriately can make some people (financiers) better-off and other people (the rest of us) wondering what exactly happened here. My hope was to show that we need to sort out when it is appropriate to use arbitrage-based techniques *before* the tools of modern finance are used to cross over into the weasel zone (or worse).

What strikes me as important to recognize is that none of this is easy. The constant barrage of financial scandals can give the impression that modern finance is at best "ethically challenged" or at worst fatally flawed. This is too harsh. People make mistakes, and even the best intentions can lead to bad outcomes.

This does not necessarily imply an ethical failure, although some people do indeed choose to act in reprehensible ways. What is more troubling is that the complexity of modern financial transactions can obscure ethical dimensions, even to the point that some practitioners may not realize that there are any ethical boundaries to consider. Certainly some of the cases we looked at seem to exhibit such ethical blindness. And, even when people are cognizant of ethical concerns, as other case studies make clear, what falls short of, or what crosses over, the lines demarcating unethical behavior is not always obvious.

How, then, to change things? Do we simply need more rules and regulations, more laws that prohibit specific practices and delineate more clearly what may not be done? In specific areas, this may be the case. Harmonizing accounting standards, banking rules, and market regulations across countries seems like a logical place to start. But, overall, I do not think "more rules" is the answer. The beauty of modern finance is that it is not limited by traditional rules and constructs—if you want something new, you can use the tools of modern finance to package cash flows to construct it, often developing new, synthetic versions of things that might currently exist. But this also means that you can circumvent rules (and prohibitions) by arbitraging around them—and the more precise the line about what is proscribed, the easier it is to construct an arbitrage-based alternative!

That does not mean, however, that finance is unstoppable, that "weasel zone" behavior is just part and parcel of how things work. There are, in my view, at least two ways in which the power of finance can be harnessed for good purposes and deflected from more unsavory pursuits. The first is to move away from explicit rules and toward more general standards. My argument here can be illustrated by the outcome in the JPMVEC California energy case. There is no question that the underlying algorithm was not "optimal" in the sense that bidding strategies like those developed by JPMVEC could exploit the system for private gain. But as CAISO discovered, changing the specific formula did not really solve the problem, because the traders at JPMVEC just developed new strategies to take advantage of the new formulas. What did ultimately stop the behavior was FERC's broad construct regarding what constituted manipulative behavior in energy markets. In effect, this manipulation standard did not outlaw particular practices but instead focused on the end result that activities could not be disruptive to the effective functioning of the electricity market.

Increasing uncertainty by moving to standards rather than to rules has some downsides—"bright lines" make it easier to see some boundaries and so give greater legal clarity. But the precision of rules can mask the reality that ethical boundaries are not always clear-cut. And the upside of standards is that without precise rules to delineate exactly what is acceptable, it becomes mathematically much harder to replicate something synthetically and thereby arbitrage around prohibitions.

This focus on the incentive problems of rules in the context of modern finance provides a new take on the ongoing (and voluminous) debate in legal circles regarding rules versus standards.[1] One aspect of this debate focuses on the role of trust (or lack thereof) in the decision-maker. As Kathleen M. Sullivan notes in the *Harvard Law Review*, "Rules embody a distrust for the decision-maker they seek to constrain."[2] Thus, when decision-makers are trustworthy, you can rely on standards; when they are not, you need rules to constrain their behavior. The recent plethora of rules in the aftermath of the financial crisis typifies this approach. From Dodd-Frank to bank secrecy and anti–money laundering, to leverage requirements, the rules are concrete and exact—and clearly consistent with the notion that banks are not to be trusted to make the right decision.

The advent of modern finance changes this debate in an interesting way. Now, while you may not view finance decision-makers as trustworthy, you can count on them to arbitrage their way around explicit rules, relying on the specificity of these rules to obviate their usefulness. In this context, the rules themselves incentivize the very untrustworthy behavior you seek to constrain. Consequently, in the era of modern finance, financial regulation may be better served by the use of standards to constrain untrustworthy decision-makers, the opposite of the conventional wisdom (and large parts of the present-day regulatory approach).

The current issues connected with some high-frequency trading activities serve as a case in point—what may be a more effective way to curb unethical behavior is not to enumerate the proscribed activities (spoofing, layering, etc.) but rather to enforce the standard that trading behavior must be consistent with promoting orderly and efficient markets. Such a focus on standards rather than on rules is in line with the more normative notion that ethics is not about determining a list of what you shouldn't do but rather about establishing norms and guidelines for what would be ethical behavior.[3]

A second, and more powerful, force that can limit the ability to arbitrage around ethical boundaries is the role played by market acceptance. Creating alternatives to particular contracts is really valuable only if you can actually sell the resulting contract to someone. The market, however, may simply not be willing to accept that the synthetic version is an ethical alternative. An interesting case in point is illustrated by "*sukuk* arbitrage" in Islamic finance. Islamic finance generally bans both the payment of interest and pure monetary speculation.[4] That has the practical implication of banning most types of bond contracts. What is permitted is sharing in the returns of underlying assets, and this has led to the development of what are termed *sukuk* financial contracts. The *sukuk* grants partial ownership of the asset to the holder, and so these are generally viewed as sharia (or Islamic law) compliant.

In 2011, Goldman Sachs attempted to enter the Islamic finance market by using financial engineering to design a $2 billion *sukuk* issuance. The particular contract Goldman created was based on a *murabaha*, or what is essentially a cost-plus-profit arrangement for investors. Like the *contractus trinus*, discussed in chapter 2, the *murabaha* uses a set of transactions to replicate what looks like a standard loan with interest (or essentially a bond).[5] For example, a commodity *murabaha* has a bank buy $10,000 worth of copper in the market; it then sells the copper to a customer for $11,000 payable at a later date; and the customer then immediately sells the copper today for $10,000. So the end result is that the customer has "borrowed" $10,000 and has to repay $11,000 (essentially the loan plus interest) at a later date.[6] The *sukuk* that Goldman designed was more complex, but the underlying idea was to use this concept to create a new type of sharia-compliant contract.

Goldman intended to list this *sukuk* on the Irish Stock Exchange, thereby giving investors a way to trade in and out of these contracts. A wrinkle here, however, is that trading at any price other than par could be viewed as violating sharia strictures against speculative trading. Goldman was able to get approval of its proposed contract by a panel of religious scholars, but the market had a different response.[7] Some objected to the after-market trading as being unacceptable, others raised concerns about the possible use of the proceeds for non-Islamic purposes, and still others questioned whether the underlying structure was actually sharia compliant in the first place. Whatever the concerns, this *sukuk* was never issued.

I have no idea whether this contract was compliant with Islamic law, but what I find interesting here is that the market (or at least the potential buyers) decided otherwise. Goldman has since tried again, coming to the Islamic finance market with a new *sukuk* structure in September 2014 that met with greater market acceptance.[8] What the original Goldman *sukuk* did succeed in doing was generate extensive discussion and debate about what constituted an acceptable contract in religious terms and that debate changed the outcome.

I think the same thing can happen with respect to the role more generally of ethics in modern financial markets. The increased focus on these issues, from regulators, journalists, boards of directors, managers, protestors, ordinary citizens, and even finance professors can lead to greater awareness, greater discussion and debate, and eventually change. What is culturally acceptable evolves over time, driven in part by exactly such debate. Perhaps like the sea change in public attitudes surrounding littering on highways or killing lions for sport in African countries, public outcry and debate can change the usage of modern finance for the better.

NOTES

Chapter 1

1. See "How Goldman Sachs Helped Greece to Mask Its True Debt," *Spiegel Online*, Feb. 8, 2010, and "Goldman Secret Greece Loan Shows Two Sinners as Client Unravels," *Bloomberg Business*, March 5, 2012.
2. As we will sort out in chapter 9, Goldman structured a currency swap with an embedded loan, allowing Greece to use favorable European rules regarding accounting for derivative contracts to seemingly reduce its indebtedness.
3. Pope Benedict XVI put it another way: "It is not the instrument that must be called to account, but individuals, their moral conscience, and their social and personal responsibility." *Caritas in Veritate* (2009), para. 36.
4. In Sept. 2013, Goldman Sachs structured the first rated securitization of solar energy globally, the JRE Mega Solar Project Bond Trust 1 ($13.5 million, twenty years, rated A to BBB+ by Japan Credit Rating Agency). Goldman noted, "This transaction has led the way to the development of a pipeline of similar project bonds to more efficiently fund renewable energy throughout Japan, and sets the stage for expanding securitization of renewable energy projects globally." For details, see http://www.goldmansachs.com/media-relations/press-releases/current/gs-targets-1billion-dollar-renewable-energy-japan.html.
5. Scott Adams, *Dilbert and the Way of the Weasel* (New York: Harper Collins, 2002).
6. Richard Posner, "Is Banking Unusually Corrupt and If So, Why?," *Becker-Posner Blog*, July 22, 2012, available at http://www.becker-posner

-blog.com/2012/07/is-banking-unusually-corrupt-and-if-so-why-posner.html.

7. James O'Toole and Warren G. Bennis, "What's Needed Next: A Culture of Candor," *Harvard Business Review*, June 2009, cited in William D. Cohan, "Can Bankers Behave?," *Atlantic*, March 2015.

8. An excellent discussion of these issues is Bjorn Bartling and Roberto A. Weber (2013), "Do Markets Erode Social Responsibility?," available at http://papers.ssrn.com/sol3/papers.cfm?abstract_id=2357561. See also Michael J. Sandel, *What Money Can't Buy: The Moral Limits of Markets* (New York: Farrar, Straus and Giroux, 2012).

9. Armin Falk and Nora Szech, "Morals and Markets," *Science* 340 (May 10, 2013): 707–11.

10. An interesting discussion of these issues is Max H. Bazerman and Ann E. Tenbrunsel, "Ethical Breakdowns," *Harvard Business Review*, April 2011. I thank my colleague Jim Detert for insightful discussions on this topic.

11. For a discussion of how individuals are more likely "to overlook dirty work that is outsourced to others," see Bazerman and Tenbrunsel, "Ethical Breakdowns," available at https://hbr.org/2011/04/ethical-breakdowns.

12. Cited in speech by William Dudley, "Enhancing Financial Stability by Improving Culture in the Financial Services Industry," Oct. 20, 2014, available at http://www.ny.frb.org/newsevents/speeches/2014/dud141020a.html.

13. See http://www.edelman.com/insights/intellectual-property/2014-edelman-trust-barometer/trust-in-business/trust-in-financial-services/. For data on the Gallup poll, see http://www.gallup.com/poll/1654/honesty-ethics-professions.aspx. I thank Roger Ferguson for suggesting these references to me.

Chapter 2

1. The Catholic Church decreed that it was morally wrong to make money from money because money per se was intrinsically unproductive. Thus, it was forbidden to charge interest on a loan of money. It was allowed, however, to receive compensation for hazards and delays in repayments, and profit sharing was also acceptable. For more discussion, see "A Distant Mirror," *Forbes*, April 21, 2008.

2. See Harris Irfan, *Heaven's Bankers* (New York: Overlook Press, 2014), p. 40, for a fascinating discussion of the role of arbitrage in Islamic finance techniques.

3. Franco Modigliani and Merton Miller, "The Cost of Capital, Corporation Finance, and the Theory of Investment," *American Economic Review* 48 (1958): 261–97. For a fuller perspective on the impact of Modigliani and Miller's work on modern finance, see Merton Miller, "The Modigliani-Miller Propositions after Thirty Years," *Journal of Economic Perspectives* 2, no. 4 (1988): 99–120.
4. This is proposition one of the Modigliani and Miller theorems.
5. The first organized options exchange, the CBOE, would start trading only in 1973, aided in part by the new research of Black, Scholes, and Merton published in 1973.
6. A European option allows these transactions only on the last day of the contract, whereas American options can be exercised anytime in the life of the contract. The following analysis is done for European options.
7. Cited in Robert A. Jarrow and Arkadev Chatterjea, *An Introduction to Derivative Securities, Financial Markets, and Risk Management* (New York: W. W. Norton, 2013), p. 397. The original quotation is from Leonard R. Higgins, *The Put-and-Call* (London: Effington Wilson, 1896), p. 26. The Higgins book is available at www.archives.org.
8. As was the case with the MM theorem, the put-call parity relation assumes no market frictions, and more complex formulations can be derived to deal with some of these imperfections.
9. Bachelier's dissertation, "The Theory of Speculation," used the concept of Brownian motion to evaluate stock options. His work, while not well received at the time, is now viewed as being the first to apply advanced mathematics to finance.
10. More precisely, there needs to be agreement on the risk premium of the stock, but no one agrees on this either.
11. My discussion here is drawn from chapter 19 of Jarrow and Chatterjea, *Introduction to Derivative Securities*. Readers interested in a complete derivation of option pricing models should consult this excellent resource on option pricing and risk management.
12. Calculating the proper hedge ratio requires entering the land of the "greeks" (the name given measures such as the delta, vega, and gamma). Suffice it to say, the exact calculation of these variables, as well as the solution to the underlying partial differential equations, requires some mathematical sophistication or, lacking that, just the ability to access a computer with preprogrammed option analytics.
13. Daily correlations were calculated for the period Aug. 15, 2014, through Aug. 14, 2015, on the basis of data from Yahoo Finance.

Chapter 3

1. This example is drawn from the appendix in Christophe Pérignon and Boris Vallée, "The Political Economy of Financial Innovation: Evidence from Local Governments," Working Paper HEC Paris (June 30, 2015), available at www.bostonfed.org/economic/conf/municipal-finance-2015/papers/vallee.pdf.
2. There are, of course, a few differences between the natural bond process and the synthetic bond process. When IBM issues a bond, it receives proceeds that can be used to fund activities, whereas in the synthetic bond what is being replicated is only the yield and not the funding aspect. But because the synthetic bond is a derivative, its value depends on the underlying actual bond, and not the other way around. If there are too many synthetics, the demand for synthetics will fall, causing them to be less valuable than the natural bond. Arbitrage will result in the creation of fewer synthetics as equilibrium with the natural bond is restored.
3. See Jonathan R. Macey, *The Death of Corporate Reputation: How Integrity Has Been Destroyed on Wall Street* (Indianapolis: FT Press, 2013), chap. 3, for a detailed analysis of the Gibson Greetings case, as well as related litigation involving Proctor & Gamble and Bankers Trust.
4. See "Blurred Vision," *Economist*, April 8, 1995. The claim is also cited in Macey, *Death of Corporate Reputation*.
5. Interestingly, Gibson actually won on this particular swap: BT paid Gibson $978,000 to terminate the swap.
6. "Bankers Trust Sued on Derivatives," *Wall Street Journal*, Sept. 13, 1994.
7. "Bankers Trust Settles Charges on Derivatives," *Wall Street Journal*, Dec. 23, 1994.

Chapter 4

1. This reply is cited in James Grant, *Money of the Mind: How the 1980s Got That Way* (New York: Farrar, Straus and Giroux, 1994). The original citation appears to be in Edward Lefevre, "Mr. Williams and the Chemical National Bank," 1902, in *World's Work* 3 (1902): 205, available at http://books.google.com/books?id=DFA5AQAAMAAJ&pg=PA2005.
2. Simon Blackburn, *Ethics: A Very Short Introduction* (Oxford: Oxford Uni-

versity Press, 2001), p. 9. Also cited at https://en.wikipedia.org/wiki/Ethics_in_religion.

3. For the quotations, see Tanenbaum Center for Interreligious Understanding at www.tanenbaum.org.

4. Francis Fukuyama, in his book *Origins of Political Order: From Prehuman Times to the French Revolution* (New York: Farrar, Straus and Giroux: 2011), provides an interesting discussion of this higher order in the context of the relation between kings, the church, and the resulting rule of law. He argues that in Europe the rule of law prevailed because even kings faced a higher law and so could be called to account for their behavior—as exemplified by Emperor Henry IV's giving in to Pope Gregory VII at Canossa. There is no rule of law in China, he writes, because there was no higher law than the emperor. I thank Michael Brennan for interesting discussion on this issue.

5. Harris Irfan, *Heaven's Bankers* (New York: Overlook Press), p. 65.

6. Ibid., p. 67.

7. Benedict XVI, *Caritas in Veritate* (2009), para. 7.

8. Ibid., para. 36.

9. See Mark Carney, "Inclusive Capitalism: Creating a Sense of the Systemic," May 27, 2014, available at http://www.bankofengland.co.uk/publications/Documents/speeches/2014/speech731.pdf.

10. See Meinhard v. Salmon, 249 NY 458, Court of Appeals, New York, argued Dec. 4, 1928, decided Dec. 31, 1928.

11. See SEC v. Chery Corp, 318 U.S. 80, 85–86 (1943).

12. See Geoffrey Hosking, review of *Why We Need a History of Trust*, in *Reviews in History*, at http://www.history.ac.uk/reviews/review/287a. These issues are treated more generally in Geoffrey Hosking, *Trust: A History* (Oxford: Oxford University Press, 2014).

13. In "Trust in Financial Markets," *European Financial Management* 14 (Sept. 2008): 617–32, Colin Meyer explores how the concept of trust is needed for the development of financial markets. Luigi Guiso, Paola Sapienza, and Luigi Zingales, in "Trusting the Stock Market," *Journal of Finance* 63, no. 6 (2008): 2557–600, show how trust influences stock market participation. See also Luigi Guiso, "A Trust-Driven Financial Crisis," European University Institute Working Paper 2010/07, which argues that unless trust is restored the move away from ambiguous securities will have adverse effects on the economy.

14. "Greed—and Fear," *Economist*, Jan. 24, 2009, p. 22.

15. See Dan M. Gallagher, "Remarks at Society of Corporate Secretaries

and Governance Professionals," July 11, 2013, available at www.sec.gov/News/Speech/Detail/Speech/1370539700301.

16. The video is available at the Department of Justice website, http://www.justice.gov/agwa.php?id=11. An interesting article on legal prosecutions in the aftermath of the financial crisis is "Why Only One Banker Went to Jail for the Financial Crisis," *New York Times*, April 30, 2014.

17. Michael Sandel, *Justice: What's the Right Thing to Do?* (New York: Farrar, Straus and Giroux, 2009).

18. This discussion is largely drawn from Andrew Yuengert, "Two Barriers to Moral Agency in Business Education," *Logos* 13, no. 3 (Summer 2010).

19. Ibid., p. 46.

20. Sandel, *Justice*, p. 105.

21. Ibid., p. 41.

22. John Stuart Mill pushed utilitarianism in this direction, arguing that it failed to respect the importance of individual rights. Mill also believed that justice as it relates to the individual is a sacred duty that cannot be traded off for the overall good.

23. This concept of improving someone's utility without reducing anyone else's is known as Pareto optimality.

24. Sandel, *Justice*, p. 111.

25. In this respect Kant's views have the same basis as Catholic social thought, which also argues for the primacy of human dignity.

26. Sandel, *Justice*, p. 111.

27. Ibid., p. 112.

28. John Rawls, *A Theory of Justice* (Cambridge: Belknap Press of Harvard University Press, 1971); Robert Nozick, *Anarchy, State, and Utopia* (New York: Basic Books, 1974). Some might also include Ayn Rand's Objectivist movement in this list, since its outlook allegedly influenced Alan Greenspan's thinking. Rand argued that her views were influenced by Aristotle, although they seem rather different to me. Discussion of the Objectivist movement can be found in *Wikipedia*, s.v. "Ayn Rand."

29. *Wikipedia*, s.v., "Ethical movement," accessed Nov. 24, 2015.

30. Ibid.

31. Ethical Culture Society of Bergen County, "Our Statement of Purpose," at http://ethicalfocus.org/our-statement-of-purpose/.

32. More precisely, the Nine Principles of Union (1912) states, "The individual considers the convictions of others but finds final authority on any opinion or action in his or her own conscientious and reasoned judgment." See ibid.

33. Quoted in "Our Statement of Purpose," at http://ethicalfocus.org/our-statement-of-purpose/.

34. The Foundation for a Better Life website, for example, features four billboards focusing on fairness. See http://www.values.com/search?utf8=%E2%9C%93&q=fairness.

Chapter 5

1. Cited in Thomas Cathcart and Daniel Klien, *Plato and a Platypus Walk into a Bar: Understanding Philosophy through Jokes* (New York: Penguin Books, 2008).
2. Albert Z. Carr, "Is Business Bluffing Ethical?," *Harvard Business Review*, Jan.–Feb. 1968.
3. Milton Friedman, *Capitalism and Freedom* (Chicago: University of Chicago Press, 1962).
4. Milton Friedman, "The Social Responsibility of Business Is to Increase Profits," *New York Times Magazine*, Sept. 13, 1970.
5. If you question whether this is actually dated, consider his statement that "many wives are not prepared to accept the fact that businesses operate with a special code of ethics" ("Is Business Bluffing Ehtical?," p. 152). Of course, an interesting question is how representative Carr's views were back then.
6. Aquinas recognized that laws coercively promote virtuous behavior, but because people were not perfect the law should prohibit only the most grievous vices. Perfection in virtue is still a goal, however, so there is virtue that must be promoted beyond that legislated in the law. See *Summa Theologica*, bk. 2, 96.2. I thank Joe Kaboski for interesting discussion on this point.
7. See Dana Radcliffe, "Should Companies Obey the Law If Breaking It Is More Profitable?," *Huffington Post*, July 5, 2012.
8. Robert Reich, *Supercapitalism: The Transformation of Business, Democracy, and Everyday Life* (New York: Alfred A. Knopf, 2007).
9. Jonathan R. Macey, *The Death of Corporate Reputation: How Integrity Has Been Destroyed on Wall Street* (Indianapolis: FT Press, 2013), p. 1.
10. Cited ibid., p. 87. See also "Buffett's 1991 Salomon Testimony," *Wall Street Journal*, May 1, 2010.
11. Alan Greenspan, congressional testimony, Oct. 22, 2008. I thank Brandon Becker for bringing this to my attention, and for interesting discussion on this general issue.
12. See, e.g., Mark Carney, "Inclusive Capitalism: Creating a Sense of the Systemic," May 27, 2014, available at http://www.bankofengland.co.uk/publications/Documents/speeches/2014/speech731.pdf. See also William Dudley, "Enhancing Financial Stability by Improving Culture in the Finan-

cial Services Industry," Oct. 20, 2014, available at http://www.ny.frb.org/newsevents/speeches/2014/dud141020a.html.

13. The classic paper on adverse selection is George Akerloff, "The Market for 'Lemons': Quality Uncertainty and the Market Mechanism," *Quarterly Journal of Economics* 84, no. 3 (Aug. 1970).

14. Cited in Michael Sandel, "Market Reasoning as Moral Reasoning: Why Economists Should Re-engage with Political Philosophy," *Journal of Economic Perspectives* 27, no. 4 (2013): 136.

15. This is the same John Nash whose life story was depicted in the movie *A Beautiful Mind*. His work is widely credited with setting the foundations of modern game theory.

16. A classic paper investigating Nash equilibria in bank runs is Douglas Diamond and Philip Dybvig, "Bank Runs, Deposit Insurance, and Liquidity," *Journal of Political Economy* 91 (June 1983).

17. A pure strategy determines the move any player will make for any situation he may face. Games can also have mixed strategies, which assign a probability to each pure strategy. In a mixed strategy, the player can randomize across strategies. For more discussion, see *Wikipedia*, s.v. "strategy (game theory)."

18. Michael Lewis, *Liar's Poker: Rising through the Wreckage on Wall Street* (New York: W. W. Norton, 1989), p. 136.

19. See Carney, "Inclusive Capitalism," pp. 3–5.

20. An objection to this approach is that it is only enlightened self-interest and that it does not give any weight to the role played by ethics in its own right.

21. See CFTC Regulation 40.6(a) Certification. Adoption of Rule 575 ("Disruptive Practices Prohibited") and Issuance of CME Group Market Regulation Advisory Notice RA1405-5. CME Submission No. 14-367, available at http://www.cftc.gov/filings/orgrules/rule082814cmedcm001.pdf.

22. Oliver Wendell Holmes Jr., "Early Forms of Liability" (lecture 1), in *The Common Law* (Boston: Little, Brown, 1909). I thank Brandon Becker for suggesting this quotation to me.

Chapter 6

1. It would also appear more profitable as its return on assets would be higher.

2. See Report of Anton R. Valukas, U.S. Bankruptcy Court, In re Lehman Brothers Holdings, Case 08-13555, March 2010.

3. Martin Kelly, controller of Lehman Brothers, apparently warned two Lehman CFOs that the lack of economic substance to Repo 105 posed reputational risks to the firm if the public found out.

4. See Report of Anton R. Valukas, discussion in pt. 3.
5. For discussion, see Matt Levine, "SEC Decides to Let Lehman Stay Dead," *Bloomberg View*, Sept. 9, 2013.
6. In April 2015 Ernst & Young also settled claims, without admitting guilt, with the New York Attorney General's Office that it allowed Lehman Brothers to mislead investors. See "Ernst & Young Reaches Settlement with N.Y. Attorney General," *Wall Street Journal*, April 15, 2015. Interestingly, the article notes that in the earlier, 2013 case, an arbitrator sided with the accounting firm, concluding that wrongdoing at the bank was "overwhelmingly attributable" to Lehman Brothers.
7. See Department of Justice, Office of Public Affairs, "Bank of America to Pay $16.65 Billion in Historic Justice Department Settlement for Financial Fraud Leading up to and during the Financial Crisis," Aug. 21, 2014, available at http://www.justice.gov/opa/pr/bank-america-pay-1665-billion-historic-justice-department-settlement-financial-fraud-leading.
8. By comparison over this period, JPMorgan Chase, Bear Stearns, and Washington Mutual together issued approximately $450 billion in MBS. The data are from "Bank of America nears $16 Billion to $17 Billion Settlement," *Wall Street Journal*, Aug. 6, 2014.
9. See annex 1, Bank of America Corporation Statement of Facts, DOJ Settlement, available at http://www.justice.gov/iso/opa/resources/4312014829141220799708.pdf, p. 3.
10. Loan categories are based on borrowers' credit scores. Currently, prime mortgage loans are made with borrowers with scores above 700, subprime to borrowers with scores below 660, and Alt-A (or Extreme Alt-A) generally to borrowers with scores between 660 and 700, although borrower credit histories can also influence their designation. For more discussion, see https://www.fdic.gov/about/comein/background.html.
11. Annex 1, Bank of America Corporation Statement of Facts, DOJ Settlement, p. 11.
12. Ibid., p. 12.
13. Ibid., p. 14.
14. Ibid., pp. 12–13.
15. Ibid., p. 10.
16. Richard Posner, "Is Banking Unusually Corrupt, and If So, Why?," *Becker-Posner Blog*, July 22, 2012, available at http://www.becker-posner-blog.com/2012/07/is-banking-unusually-corrupt-and-if-so-why-posner.html.
17. Ibid. See also Neil Irwin, "Why Can't the Banking Industry Solve Its Ethics Problem?," *New York Times*, July 29, 2014.

18. Max H. Bazerman and Ann E. Tenbrunsel, "Ethical Breakdowns," *Harvard Business Review*, April 2011.
19. See "Judge Orders Bank of America to Pay $1.27 Billion in 'Hustle' Case," *Wall Street Journal*, July 30, 2014.
20. The Appeals Court overturned the verdict of fraud, finding that "willful but silent noncompliance" was a breach of contract but not fraud per se, a distinction that illustrates the challenges of using a pure legal standard to define poor behavior. See " 'Hustle' Mortgage Fraud Case Falls Into Crevice of the Law," *New York Times*, May 31, 2016.
21. See "SEC Charges Goldman Sachs with Fraud in Structuring and Marketing of CDO Tied to Subprime Mortgages," April 16, 2010, available at http://www.sec.gov/news/press/2010/2010-59.htm.
22. A CDO can have as collateral a wide variety of debt instruments, including mortgages, loans, and bonds. In the Abacus case, the underlying collateral are tranches of mortgage-backed securities.
23. See "SEC Charges Goldman."
24. "Abacus Deal: As Bad as They Come," *Wall Street Journal*, April 20, 2010.
25. For details of the complaint, see SEC Litigation Release No. 21489, available at http://www.sec.gov/litigation/litreleases/2010/lr21489.htm.
26. See "SEC Charges Goldman."
27. U.S. District Court Southern District of New York, Consent of Defendant Goldman, Sachs & Co., 10-CV-3229 (BSJ), found at http://www.sec.gov/litigation/litreleases/2010/consent-pr2010-123.pdf.
28. See "Goldman Settles Its Battle with the SEC," *Wall Street Journal*, July 16, 2010.
29. For discussion, see "Abacus Deal: As Bad as They Come."
30. See SEC Complaint, available at http://www.sec.gov/litigation/complaints/2010/comp-pr2010-59.pdf, para. 18.
31. For discussion, see Francesco Gino, Don A. Moore, and Max Bazerman, "See No Evil: When We Overlook Other People's Unethical Behavior," in *Social Decision Making: Social Dilemmas, Social Values, and Ethical Judgments*, ed. R. M. Kramer et al. (London: Routledge, 2010).

Chapter 7

1. Peter Chapman, "Before the Fall: Bernard L. Madoff," *Traders Magazine*, March 2009, pp. 31–32. Much of the discussion here is drawn from this excellent article.

2. Rule 390 applied to any NYSE stock listed before April 26, 1979. This rule was intended to stop dealers from internalizing order flow, and so was widely viewed as an anticompetitive measure.
3. Chapman, "Before the Fall," p. 42.
4. The Cincinnati Stock Exchange has a colorful history, and interested readers will find information at http://www.cincinnatistockexchange.us/cincinnati-stock-exchange-timeline/. After becoming an electronic exchange, the CSE was not actually in Cincinnati, having based its computers in Chicago. The CSE was subsequently renamed the National Stock Exchange, which in turn ceased trading in May 2014. It may still live again, for the NSX was recently sold to Open Match Holdings. See "Fuld Advises on Deal to Buy National Stock Exchange," *Wall Street Journal*, Oct. 9, 2014.
5. There is academic research showing that Madoff was successful in reducing the adverse selection in the orders executing in Cincinnati relative to those in New York. See David Easley, Nicholas M. Kiefer, and Maureen O'Hara, "Cream-Skimming or Profit-Sharing? The Curious Role of Purchased Order Flow," *Journal of Finance* 51 (July 1996): 811–33. See also Robert H. Battalio, "Third Market Broker-Dealers: Cost Competitors or Cream Skimmers?," ibid., 52 (March 1997): 341–52.
6. See "JPMorgan to Pay $410 Million to Settle Power Probes," *Financial Times*, July 30, 2013.
7. 144 FERC (61,068) In Re Make-Whole Payments and Related Bidding Strategies, Order Approving Stipulation and Consent Agreement, July 30, 2013, available at http://www.ferc.gov/CalendarFiles/20130730080931-IN11-8-000.pdf, p. 14.
8. For an extensive discussion of electricity markets, see FERC, *Energy Primer: A Handbook of Energy Market Basics*, Nov. 2015, available at https://www.ferc.gov/market-oversight/guide/energy-primer.pdf.
9. See U.S. Senate Permanent Subcommittee on Investigations, *Wall Street Bank Involvement with Physical Commodities*, Nov. 20 and 21 hearings, p. 321.
10. Ibid., p. 322.
11. Ibid., p. 344 n2245.
12. Ibid., p. 343.
13. 144 FERC (61,068) In Re Make-Whole Payments, pp. 10–11.
14. This example is drawn from "Prepared Direct Testimony of Mr. Mark Rothleder," available at http://www.caiso.com/Documents/March25_2011Errata-March18_2011TariffAmendment-ModifyMarketSettlementRulesinDocketNo_ER11-3149-000.pdf, pp. 14–15.
15. 144 FERC (61,068) In Re Make-Whole Payments, p. 7, para. 41.

16. Cited in *Wall Street Bank Involvement with Physical Commodities*, p. 342.
17. See "Prepared Direct Testimony of Mr. Mark Rothleder," in CAISO Docket Nos. ER11-3149-000, available at http://www.caiso.com/2b45/2b45d10069e0.pdf, p. 19, fig. 2.
18. Ibid., p. 17.
19. Letter of March 25, 2011, Re: CAISO Docket Nos. ER11-3149-000 Tariff Revision and Request for Expedited Treatment, available at http://www.caiso.com/documents/march25_2011errata-march18_2011 tariffamendment-modifymarketsettlementrulesindocketno_er11-3149 -000.pdf.
20. Cited in *Wall Street Bank Involvement with Physical Commodities*, p. 341.
21. Order Approving Stipulation and Consent Agreement, available at http://www.ferc.gov/CalendarFiles/20130730080931-IN11-8-000.pdf, p. 13.
22. Ibid., pp. 14–15.
23. David Kocieniewski, "A Shuffle of Aluminum, But to Banks, Pure Gold," *New York Times*, July 20, 2013.
24. *Wall Street Bank Involvement with Physical Commodities*, p. 221.
25. "Statement of Goldman Sachs: Background and Facts on Financial Intermediation, Certain Investments and Risk Management in the Commodities Markets, November 19, 2014," available at http://www .goldmansachs.com/media-relations/in-the-news/current/commodities -markets-and-financial-intermediation.pdf, pp. 13, 25.
26. A LME warrant conveys title to a specific lot of 25 metric tons of "high grade primary aluminum" stored in an LME-approved warehouse. See *Wall Street Bank Involvement with Physical Commodities*, p. 175.
27. Ibid., p. 187.
28. "Statement of Goldman Sachs," pp. 27–28 for discussion of prebates and other incentives.
29. The LME would raise this to 3,000 tons a day in 2013.
30. *Wall Street Bank Involvement with Physical Commodities*, pp. 195–96.
31. Over time, the deals got even better. Red Kite negotiated three deals in 2012 and 2013 giving it (i) a day-one cash incentive when the warrants were canceled; (ii) a period of free rent; and (iii) another cash incentive for re-warranting. See ibid., p. 199.
32. Alternatively, you could try to deliver the warranted aluminum as settlement of a futures contract, in which case the storage rent and queue became someone else's problem.
33. See Matt Levine, "The Goldman Sachs Aluminum Conspiracy Was Pretty Silly," *Bloomberg View*, Nov. 20, 2014.
34. "Statement of Goldman Sachs," p. 2.

35. *Wall Street Bank Involvement with Physical Commodities*, p. 204.
36. Because the metal in these warehouses was used primarily to meet obligations arising from trading activity, holders of a long futures contract opting to take delivery would receive warrants in settlement of futures contracts, making them a new Metro client. Lucky them! In only two short years they could get their aluminum out (and in the meantime keep sending those rent checks).
37. *Wall Street Bank Involvement with Physical Commodities*, pp. 171–72.
38. Levine, "Goldman Sachs Aluminum Conspiracy."
39. Interestingly, Goldman did note that "the length of a queue may impact LME spot prices," consistent with queue length potentially affecting hedge effectiveness. See "Statement of Goldman Sachs," p. 28.
40. *Wall Street Bank Involvement with Physical Commodities*, p. 180.
41. See "Statement of Goldman Sachs," p. 26.

Chapter 8

1. A nice introduction to high-frequency trading can be found in the Foresight Project, the British government's study of the high-frequency world, available at https://www.gov.uk/government/collections/future-of-computer-trading. For a more advanced analysis, see David Easley, Marcos López de Prado, and Maureen O'Hara, *High-Frequency Trading: New Realities for Traders, Markets and Regulators* (London: Risk Books, 2014).
2. See *Wikepedia*, s.v. "algorithm."
3. Note that this strategy is self-financing because you can use the money you get selling the higher-priced stock A to buy the lower-priced stock B.
4. See SEC Market Analysis, "Equity Market Speed Relative to Order Placement," March 19, 2014, available at http://www.sec.gov/marketstructure/research/highlight-2014-02.html#.VSa_7_nF98E. See also G. E. Berman, "What Drives the Complexity and Speed of Our Markets?," April 14, 2014, available at http://www.sec.gov/News/Speech/Detail/Speech/1370541505819#.VSa_AfnF98E.
5. This is essentially what Michael Lewis claimed in his much discussed book *Flash Boys: A Wall Street Revolt* (New York: W. W. Norton, 2014). The argument is that a new kind of "electronic front running" occurs because HF traders use proprietary data to see trades before others who get their information from the consolidated tape. I believe this is an incorrect expansion of front running because, unlike the broker, the HF traders have no obligations to the traders whose trades they observe.

6. For more discussion of such behavior, see Maureen O'Hara, "What Is a Quote?," *Journal of Trading* 5, no. 2, (Spring 2010): 11–16.
7. Scott Patterson, "Regulators Target Day-Trading Firm," *Wall Street Journal*, July 30, 2012.
8. Specifically, sec. 747 of the Dodd-Frank Act prohibits disruptive practices: "It shall be unlawful for any person to engage in any trading, practice, or conduct on or subject to the rules of an registered entity that (A) violates bids or offers; (B) demonstrates intentional or reckless disregard for the orderly execution of transactions during the closing period: or (C) is of the character of, or is commonly known to the trade as, 'spoofing'. . . ."
9. For discussion of these strategies, see "Spoofing Trial Gets Testy: 'I'm Not Dealing Hot Dogs, I'm Dealing Futures,'" *Chicago Tribune*, Oct. 30, 2015.
10. See *USA v. Coscia*, 14 CR. 551, United States District Court, Northern District of Illinois, Eastern Division.
11. Kim Janssen, "CME Trader Found Guilty in Landmark 'Spoofing' Case," *Chicago Tribune*, Nov. 3, 2015.
12. See "Day-Trading Firm Fined over Manipulative Dealings," *Wall Street Journal*, Sept. 25, 2012.
13. See "Regulators Target Day-Trading Firm," *Wall Street Journal*, July 30, 2012.
14. The defendant is not named, because trading on futures exchanges is anonymous to other traders, but the identity of all parties to a trade is known by the exchange. Presumably, the lawsuit will seek to find the identity of the counterparty, which HTG argues is likely one firm. For details, see "Parasite Turns On Parasite: HFT Sues Other HFTs for 'Egregious Manipulation' of Treasury Securities," March 13, 2015, in *Zero Hedge*, available at http://www.zerohedge.com/news/2015-03-12/parasite-turns-parasite-hft-sues-other-hfts-egregious-manipulation-treasury-securiti.
15. See "SEC Charges New York-Based High Frequency Trading Firm with Fraudulent Trading to Manipulate Closing Prices," Oct. 16, 2014, available at http://www.sec.gov/News/PressRelease/Detail/PressRelease/1370543184457.
16. A good discussion of these issues is CME Group, CME Submission No. 14-367 (to the CFTC) Aug. 28, 2014.
17. An interesting discussion of these issues can be found in "Why High-Frequency Trading Is So Hard to Regulate," *New York Times*, Oct. 20, 2014.
18. See, e.g., "'Flash Crash' Charges Files," *Wall Street Journal*, April 22,

2015. Whether Sarao's trades caused, or more likely contributed to, the "flash crash" is a topic of lively debate. See, e.g., "Flash Crash Spoofer: Questions, More Questions, and Some Possible Answers," *TABB Forum*, April 23, 2015.

19. See United States of America v. Navinder Singh Sarao, U.S. District Court Northern District of Illinois Eastern Division, Case Number 15CR75, p. 6.

20. Ibid., p. 7.

21. The discussion here is largely drawn from chapter 1 of this book. See David Leinweber, *Nerds on Wall Street: Math, Machines, and Wired Markets* (Hoboken, NJ: John Wiley, 2009).

22. The telegraph was actually invented in 1837, but in those days it took time for technological advances to take hold.

23. For details, see http://www.extremetech.com/extreme/176551-new-laser-network-between-nyse-and-nasdaq-will-allow-high-frequency-traders-to-make-even-more-money.

24. Details can be found at http://www.themeparkinsider.com/flume/201310/3729/.

25. Leinweber, *Nerds on Wall Street*, p. 72.

26. Suffice it to say that every philosopher since then has also weighed in on the subject; perhaps the most influential recent perspective is in John Rawls, *A Theory of Justice* (Cambridge: Belknap Press of Harvard University Press, 1971).

27. See http://www.scu.edu/ethics/practicing/decision/justice.html#sthash.jiqRw5fg.dpuf. This article gives an excellent overview of the many complex dimensions of fairness (and the related concept of justice).

28. Manuel Velasquez, Claire Andre, Thomas Shanks, and Michael J. Meyer, "Thinking Ethically: A Framework for Making Moral Decision Making," at http://www.scu.edu/ethics/practicing/decision/thinking.html.

29. Cited in "SEC Charges Direct Edge Exchanges with Failing to Properly Describe Order Types," Jan. 12, 2015, available at http://www.sec.gov/news/pressrelease/2015-2.html.

30. Brody Mullins et al., "Traders Pay for an Early Peek at Key Data," *Wall Street Journal*, June 12, 2013.

31. Cited ibid.

32. Cited ibid.

33. See "Bloomberg to Release U-M Surveys of Consumers Starting in 2015," Oct. 7, 2014, available at http://ns.umich.edu/new/releases/22427-bloomberg-to-release-u-m-surveys-of-consumers-starting-in-2015.

34. It may also illustrate the blurring of lines between the profit and the

nonprofit activities of universities. For-profit subsidiaries are now a fact of life at major research universities, raising anew questions about the role and mission of university activities.

35. Using data from S&P 500 futures markets, Grace Xing Hu, Jun Pan, and Jiang Wang found that virtually all of the information in the release was impounded into prices in 14 to 16 milliseconds following the release at 9:54:58. Hence, even those receiving the "early" feed at 9:55 were scooped by the even earlier feed. See Jiang Wang, "Early Peek Advantage?" MIT Sloan, Finance Group, Finance Matters, blog post of May 28, 2014.

36. Business Wire, a company that distributes corporate news releases, has also agreed to stop early delivery of such information to high-frequency traders. See Ryan Tracy and Scott Patterson, "Fast Traders Are Getting Data from SEC Seconds Early," *Wall Street Journal*, Oct. 28, 2014.

37. Rogers, Skinner, and Zechman, "Run EDGAR Run: SEC Dissemination in a High-Frequency World," Chicago Booth Research Paper No. 14-36, available at http://papers.ssrn.com/sol3/Papers.cfm?abstract_id=2513350.

38. Cited in Tracy and Patterson, "Fast Traders."

39. Ibid. See also "The Investor's Advocate: How the SEC Protects Investors, Maintains Market Integrity, and Facilitates Capital Formation," at http://www.sec.gov/about/whatwedo.shtml.

40. Quotations are taken from "SEC Charges New York Stock Exchange for Improper Distribution of Market Data" 2012-189, Sept. 14, 2012, available at http://www.sec.gov/News/PressRelease/Detail/PressRelease1365171.

41. This language comes from Rule 603(a) of Reg. NMS. For an interesting discussion of these issues, see Merritt B. Fox, Lawrence R. Glosten, and Gabriel V. Rauterberg, "The New Stock Market: Sense and Nonsense," *Duke Law Journal* 65, no. 2 (Nov. 2015): 191–277.

42. For details, see http://www.nbclosangeles.com/news/local/Disneyland-Disabled-No-Longer-Skip-Lines-224810762.html.

Chapter 9

1. Dexia Group was a Belgian financial institution that required a bailout from the Belgian government during the financial crisis in 2008. Problems at the bank continued, culminating during the sovereign debt crisis in 2011 with the bank's sale to the Belgian government. At that time, the

bank was placed in an "orderly resolution" to wind down the operations of the bank, a process that is still ongoing. For more details, see http://www.dexia.com/EN/the_group/profile/Pages/default.aspx.

2. See appendix, p. 48, in Christophe Pérignon and Boris Vallée, "The Political Economy of Financial Innovation: Evidence from Local Governments," Working Paper HEC Paris (June 30, 2015), available at www.bostonfed.org/economic/conf/municipal-finance-2015/papers/vallee.pdf.

3. Pérignon and Vallée note that "in many countries, government accounting standards do not even require the disclosure of derivative transactions." Ibid., p. 9.

4. "Defending the French Municipalities against the 'Toxic Loans' of Dexia Bank," at newparadigm.schillerinstitute.com.

5. "Saint-Etienne's Swaps Explode As Financial Weapons Ambush Europe," *Business Week*, April 14, 2010.

6. "Swiss Move Leaves Small French Towns with Heavier Toxic Debt," *Bloomberg Business*, Jan. 21, 2015.

7. "French Towns Launch Debt Strike over 'Toxic' Dexia Loans," Reuters, Oct. 12, 2012.

8. Ibid., p. 4.

9. Data on structured loan usage are cited from Pérignon and Vallée, "The Political Economy of Financial Innovation," p. 3.

10. It would seem that one could solve the problem by implementing suitability rules for municipalities in France. Crafting suitability rules to prevent all stupid borrowing by local governments, however, is not always easy, as was shown by the municipal default of Orange County, California, in 1994. For a discussion of these issues, see Philippe Jorion, *Big Bets Gone Bad: Derivatives and Bankruptcy in Orange County* (San Diego: Academic Press, 1995). A more recent example of municipal default is Jefferson County, Alabama, whose 2013 bankruptcy resulted from excess borrowing for a sewer system. See in re Jefferson County, 11-bk-05736, U.S. Bankruptcy Court, Northern District of Alabama (Birmingham). For discussion, see http://www.bloomberg.com/news/articles/2013-11-22/jefferson-county-s-bankruptcy-left-few-winners-as-debt-forgiven.

11. Greece officially entered the eurozone on June 19, 2000. Its total debt levels exceeded the Maastricht levels, but its deficit levels appeared to be compliant.

12. According to Nicholas Dunbar and Elisa Martinuzzi, "Goldman Secret Greece Loan Shows Two Sinners as Client Unravels," *Bloomberg Business*, March 5, 2012, "Bloomberg News filed a lawsuit with the EU's

General Court seeking disclosure of European Central Bank documents on Greece's use of derivatives to hide loans," but those efforts were unsuccessful.

13. Ibid.

14. "Goldman Sachs Transactions with Greece," at http://www.goldmansachs.com/media-relations/in-the-news/archive/greece.html.

15. Ibid.

16. A related problem arose with respect to securitized asset sales, by which various European countries also reduced their official debt. Greece, for example, securitized its airport and highways as a way to raise funds. As Eurostat noted in 2008, "in a number of instances, the observed securitization operations seem to have been purportedly designed to achieve a given accounting result, irrespective of the economic merit of the operation." Quoted in "Wall Street Helped to Mask Debt Fueling Europe's Crisis," *New York Times*, Feb. 14, 2010.

17. See Francesca Gino, Don A. Moore, and Max H. Bazerman, "See No Evil: When We Overlook Other People's Unethical Behavior," in *Social Decision Making: Social Dilemmas, Social Values, and Ethical Judgments*, ed. R. M. Kramer et al. (London: Routledge, 2010), chap. 10.

Chapter 10

1. See the cartoon labeled "Arbitrage," at http://xcd.com/1499/.

2. An excellent article discussing these issues is Francesca Gino, Don A. Moore, and Max H. Bazerman, "See No Evil: When We Overlook Other People's Unethical Behavior," in *Social Decision Making: Social Dilemmas, Social Values, and Ethical Judgments*, ed. R. M. Kramer et al. (London: Routledge, 2010). See also David M. Messick and Max H. Bazerman, "Ethical Leadership and the Psychology of Decision Making," *Sloan Management Review* 37, no. 2 (1996); Nicholas Epley and Eugene M. Caruso, "Egocentric Ethics," *Social Justice Research* 17, no. 2 (2004); and Rebecca K. Ratner and Dale T. Miller, "The Norm of Self-interest and Its Effects on Social Action," *Journal of Personality and Social Psychology* 81, no. 1 (2001).

3. Albert Bandura, *Social Foundations of Thought and Action: A Social Cognitive Theory* (Englewood Cliffs, NJ: Prentice-Hall, 1986). For further discussion, see Albert Bandura, "Moral Disengagement in the Preparation of Inhumanities," *Personal and Social Psychology Review* 3 (1999).

4. James R. Detert, Linda K. Treviño, and Vicki L. Sweitzer, "Moral

Disengagement in Ethical Decision Making: A Study of Antecedents and Outcomes," *Journal of Applied Psychology* 93, no. 2 (2008): 375.

5. In particular, Milgram found that the people would willingly inflict pain on subjects if they were told to do so by someone in charge. See Stanley Milgram, *Obedience to Authority: An Experimental View* (New York: Harper & Row, 1974).

6. David Hume, *An Enquiry concerning the Human Understanding, and An Enquiry concerning the Principles of Morals*, ed. L. A. Selby-Bigge (Oxford: Clarendon Press, 1894).

7. See Max H. Bazerman and Ann E. Tenbrunsel, "Ethical Breakdowns," *Harvard Business Review*, April 2011.

8. The omission bias is usually explained in the context of the "trolley problem," in which an out-of-control trolley will kill for sure five people on a track or will kill one person if you divert the trolley to a different track. The ethics question is whether intervening is the moral decision or not. See Michael J. Sandel, *What Money Can't Buy: The Moral Limits of Markets* (New York: Farrar, Straus and Giroux, 2012), chap. 10, or Mark Spranca, Elisa Minsk, and Jonathan Baron, "Omission and Commission in Judgment and Choice," *Journal of Experimental Social Psychology* 27, no. 1 (1991).

9. Ilana Ritov and Jonathan Baron, "Reluctance to Vaccinate: Omission Bias and Ambiguity," *Journal of Behavioral Decision Making* 3 (1990): 263–77.

10. Neeru Paharia, Karim S. Kassam, Joshua D. Greene, and Mark H. Bazerman, "Dirty Work, Clean Hands: The Moral Psychology of Indirect Agency," *Organizational Behavior and Human Decision Processes* 109, no. 2 (2009): 136.

11. "Pharmaceutical Companies Buy Rivals' Drugs, Then Jack Up the Prices," *Wall Street Journal*, April 26, 2015.

12. Data are taken from table 3.1 in Jacopo Carmassi and Richard Herring, "The Corporate Complexity of Systemically Important Banks," *Journal of Financial Services Research*, forthcoming 2015.

13. Bazerman and Tenbrunsal, "Ethical Breakdowns," *Harvard Business Review*, April 2011.

14. David T. Welsh, Lisa D. Ordóñez, Deirdre G. Snyder, and Michael S. Christian, "The Slippery Slope: How Small Ethical Transgressions Pave the Way for Larger Future Transgressions," *Journal of Applied Psychology* 100, no. 1 (2015): 114–27.

15. Max H. Bazerman et al., "Why Good Accountants Do Bad Audits," *Harvard Business Review*, Nov. 2002.

16. William Dudley, "Enhancing Financial Stability by Improving Culture

in the Financial Services Industry," Oct. 20, 2014, available at https://www.newyorkfed.org/newsevents/speeches/2014/dud141020a.html.

17. Mark Carney, "Inclusive Capitalism: Creating a Sense of the Systemic," May 27, 2014, available at http://www.bankofengland.co.uk/publications/Documents/speeches/2014/speech731.pdf, p. 7.

18. Christine Lagarde, "Economic Inclusion and Financial Integrity," May 27, 2014, available at http://www.imf.org/external/np/speeches/2014/052714.htm.

19. Justin Welby, "Archbishop's Statement on the Future of Banking Standards," June 24, 2014, available at http://www.archbishopofcanterbury.org/articles.php/5353/archbishops-lecture-on-the-future-of-banking-standards.

20. Dudley, "Enhancing Financial Stability."

21. William D. Cohan, "Can Bankers Behave?," *Atlantic*, May 2015.

22. Linda K. Treviño is generally credited with introducing the concept of ethical culture to the academic literature on management, in her paper "Ethical Decision Making in Organizations: A Person-Situation Interactionist Model," *Academy of Management Review* 11, no. 3 (1986): 601–17.

23. Sean R. Martin, Jennifer Kish-Gephart, and James R. Detert, "Blind Forces: Ethical Infrastructure and Moral Disengagement in Organizations," *Organizational Psychology Review* 4, no. 4 (2014): 298.

24. Peter J. Henning, "The Litigation That Haunts Goldman Sachs," *New York Times*, June 25, 2012. See also Jonathan Macey, *The Death of Corporate Reputation: How Integrity Has Been Destroyed on Wall Street* (Indianapolis: FT Press, 2013), chap. 10, for a discussion of this case.

25. Cited in Richard Lambert, Banking Standards Review, May 19, 2014, p. 13.

26. Lagarde, "Economic Inclusion and Financial Integrity."

27. Dudely, "Enhancing Financial Stability."

28. Cited in Andrew Ross Sorkin, "On Wall Street, a Culture of Greed Won't Let Go," *New York Times*, July 15, 2013.

29. Labaton Sucharow, "The Street, the Bull, and the Crisis: A Survey of the US & UK Financial Services Industry," May 2015, available at www.secwhistlebloweradvocate.com/LiteratureRetrieve.aspx?ID=224757. Among the more disturbing findings in this report is that 32 percent of respondents in the UK would likely engage in insider trading to earn $10 million if they would not get caught, while 24 percent of U.S. respondents would do so.

30. Lambert, Banking Standards Review, p. 6.

31. James O'Toole and Warren G. Bennis, "What's Needed Next: A Culture of Candor," *Harvard Business Review*, June 2009.

32. GAO, "Securities and Exchange Commission: Improving Personnel Management Is Crucial for Agency's Effectiveness," GAO-13-621, July 2013, available at http://www.gao.gov/assets/660/655989.pdf. For an interesting discussion of this issue, and more generally the issues of culture in financial firms, see Andrew Lo, "The Gordon Gecko Effect: The Role of Culture in the Financial Industry," Working Paper MIT, April 2015.
33. GAO, "Securities and Exchange Commission," pp. 16–17.
34. Carney, "Inclusive Capitalism," pp. 3, 8.
35. As *Bloomberg Business* reports, the Netherlands may be particularly sensitive to these ethical issues in banking, given that the country spent 95 million euros to bail out Dutch banks during the financial crisis. See http://www.bloomberg.com/news/articles/2014-02-05/dutch-bankers-swear-to-god-as-trust-in-lenders-slumps-to-record.
36. Justin Fox, "Time for Bankers to Start Swearing," *Bloomberg View*, April 1, 2015, available at http://www.bloombergview.com/articles/2015-04-01/dutch-bankers-start-taking-an-oath-to-behave-better.
37. Ibid.
38. For perspectives on this, see David Brooks, "Becoming a Real Person," *New York Times*, Sept. 8, 2014, and Peter Steinfels, "Beliefs: The University's Role in Instilling a Moral Code among Students? None Whatever, Some Argue," ibid., June 19, 2004.
39. See the complete oath at http://mbaoath.org/about/the-mba-oath/.
40. Luigi Zingales, "Does Finance Benefit Society?," *Journal of Finance*, forthcoming. Interestingly, these issues have a longer history in economics, where some have questioned whether studying economics makes people more selfish. Robert Frank, for example, provides intriguing evidence that studying economics reduces cooperation and generosity. See http://www.gnu.org/philosophy/economics_frank/frank.html. For an informal review of this literature, see http://standupeconomist.com/are-economists-selfish-a-lit-review/.
41. William G. Christie and Paul H. Schultz, "Why Do NASDAQ Market Makers Avoid Odd-Eighth Quotes?," *Journal of Finance* 49, no. 5 (1994): 1813–40; David Yermack, "Good Timing: CEO Stock Option Awards and Company News Announcements," ibid., 52, no. 2 (1997): 449–76; and Luigi Guiso, Paola Sapienza, and Luigi Zingales, "The Value of Corporate Culture," *Journal of Financial Economics*, forthcoming.
42. Aristotle, *Nicomachean Ethics*, bk. 2, chap. 1, pp. 1103a–1103b, cited in Sandel, *What Money Can't Buy*, p. 137.

Chapter 11

1. A classic work in this area is Louis Kaplan, "Rules versus Standards: An Economic Analysis," *Duke Law Journal* 42 (1992): 557–629. A more recent discussion is Gideon Parchomovsky and Alex Stein, "Essay: Catalogs," *Columbia Law Review* 115 (2015).
2. Kathleen M. Sullivan, "The Supreme Court 1991 Term: Foreword: The Justices of Rules and Standards," *Harvard Law Review* 106, no. 22 (Nov. 1992): 17. I thank Thomas Noone for suggesting this point to me.
3. The CFA Institute's Code of Ethics and Standards of Professional Conduct is one such example of a standards-based approach. For a discussion of these normative issues, see chapter 1 in Thomas Oberlechner, "The Psychology of Ethics in the Finance and Investment Industry," CFA Institute, 2007, available at http://www.cfapubs.org/doi/pdf/10.2470/rf.v2007.n2.4697.
4. An excellent resource on Islamic finance is Harris Irfan, *Heaven's Bankers* (New York: Overlook Press, 2014). For a succinct discussion of *sukuk* contracts, see http://www.dummies.com/how-to/content/how-sukuk-islamic-bonds-differ-from-conventional-b.navId-814096.html?print=true.
5. The Institute of Islamic Banking and Insurance estimates that 80–90 percent of financial operations of some Islamic banks are based on *murabaha*. My discussion here draws from explanations available at http://www.islamic-banking.com/murabaha_sruling.aspx.
6. Technically, it is a bit more complicated. The Institute of Islamic Banking and Insurance explains, "The whole of Murabaha transaction is to be completed in two stages. In the first stage, the client requests the bank to undertake a Murabaha transaction and promises to buy the commodity specified by him, if the bank acquires the same commodity. Of course, the promise is not a legal binding. The client may go back on his promise and the bank risks the loss of the amount it has spent. In the second stage, the client purchases the good acquired by the bank on a deferred payments basis and agrees to a payment schedule. Another important requirement of Murabaha sale is that two sale contracts, one through which the bank acquires the commodity and the other through which it sells it to the client should be separate and real transactions."
7. For details, see Anjuli Davies, "Islamic Finance: Islamic Sukuk by Goldman Sachs Causes Debate," Reuters, posted Feb. 23, 2012, available at

http://www.huffingtonpost.com/2012/02/23/refile-debate-rages-over-_n_1296351.html.

8. For a discussion of the 2014 Goldman *sukuk*, see "Goldman Sachs Plans Debut Sukuk Issue as Islamic Finance Goes Mainstream," available at http://www.reuters.com/article/us-goldman-sukuk-idUSKBN0GZ1CM20140904, and "Goldman Sukuk Lures Mideast's Top Fund Manager: Islamic Finance," *Bloomberg Business*, Sept. 8, 2014.

INDEX